Finn Rasmussen

Gold Horns

Life and Religion of the Anglo-Saxons

First published in the United Kingdom in 2022 by
The Cloister House Press

ISBN 978-1-913460-54-9

Contents

Introduction

The two golden horns from Gallehus are one of the most precious finds from Danish antiquity.

They are decorated with hundreds of mysterious figures and symbols, which provide unique information on Germanic religion and social life. They also throw light on the mysterious origin of the runic alphabet. The Golden Horns were the catalyst for me beginning my study of Germanic religion.

Ever since the Gold Horns of Gallehus appeared, there have been hundreds of different explanations offered for the figures and symbols on the horns. Some have tried to find connections to Christianity. However, this theory was short-lived as the horns were buried about AD 420 and, at that time, Christianity was not known to the Germanic tribes. Another theory saw a connection to Old Norse mythology, but this theory also fell short as the gods, Thor and Odin, from Norse mythology were not worshipped in Jutland until the Viking Age, AD 750-1050.

Fifty years ago, historians of religion stated that the Gold Horns had pictures of the Divine Twins (Ward 1968), which would mean that some Germanic tribes worshipped these gods. However, no examination of the many symbols of the horns was carried out. Moreover, no thorough study has been made to date of the many picture symbols on finds from the Germanic culture.

The exceptional runic inscription on the short horn and other circumstances surrounding the finding of the horns makes it probable that the horns were sacrificed and buried when a group of Angles migrated from southern Jutland to England. This idea led me to the study of the mass migration of Angles from southern Jutland to England. The Old English poem, *Beowulf*, provides an excellent description of the situation in southern Jutland around AD 500. With the help of this and other sources, it is possible to identify different ethnic groups in southern Jutland and follow their migration routes.

The first half of this book is a description of the cultural and social life of the Germanic peoples before they left the Continent and after they invaded England. We now call the Germanic settlers in England Anglo-Saxons, but it is important to note that "Angles" and "Saxons" are not in themselves names of ethnic groups, rather the two terms were how contemporary British monks described the Germanic invaders. Thus, also included in the first part of the book is an original analysis of the archaeological finds and documentation of the Anglo-Saxon settlement.

This is then followed by a description of the religious ideas of the Germanic tribes. We will see that these ideas were very much the same for all Germanic peoples, including the Anglo-Saxons. Their religious ideas were based on three key gods, who will be described with documented analysis from the picture symbols on archaeological finds.

What makes the interpretation of the horns difficult is the fact that there are no written testimonies from the Germanic tribes themselves. When studying prehistoric symbols, the approach is often to observe the context of the symbol and then compare that symbol with similar symbols from other finds. I have used this method for the hundreds of symbols on the Gold Horns and published the result (Rasmussen 1990). This book expands on those results, but I do not go into detail on all the symbols. Instead, I concentrate on explaining the general ideas and story of the horns.

The period AD 1-400 is known as the Roman Iron Age and the period AD 400-750, the Germanic Iron Age in Denmark. I will use the term "Germanic Age" for the entire period and the term "Germanics" for all the tribes in Europe who spoke a Germanic language as the modern term, "Germans" would be misleading. In Germanic tribal society, social status was based on lineage. The chieftain or the king did not have a strong power base. In the later Germanic Age, the core power of the king increased. This change in the social system was accompanied by two new religions: Christianity in England and the Old Norse mythology in the Nordic countries.

I would like to thank my daughter Ulla Rasmussen for reading and correcting the manuscript. I also thank editor Sinéad Quirke Køngerskov for revising the manuscript from an archaeological point of view, and Thyra Johannesen for layout and cover.

The manuscript was finished in 2018.

The Find

Rarely has any other historic Danish find evoked so much excitement in the minds of both researchers and ordinary people as the Gold Horns. The horns were found in a field in the village Gallehus in southern Jutland. The story of their find has almost become folklore. One day, in the summer of 1639, a poor orphan lace maker was walking to town in order to sell her lace when she tumbled over the longer horn, which was protruding from the path. She stooped to examine what she had mistaken for a tree root. The horn eventually reached the lawful owner of all treasure: the king, Christian IV. The girl was rewarded with a new skirt. The king had the narrow end of the horn plugged with a screw plug, and gifted it to his eldest son as a drinking horn. In 1641, a drawing of the horn was made by Ole Worm (Olaus Wormius), personal physician to Christian IV. Ole Worm was not only a professor of anatomy and a very skilled artist, particularly of antiquities, he is also considered the father of Archaeology in Denmark. Ole Worm's sketch is the only known documentation of the decoration on the long horn.

A hundred years later, when digging for clay to daub his cottage, a small farmer from Gallehus found the shorter horn, only a few paces from where the first one had been found, but a couple of spits deeper. This horn was shorter as only the broad part had been preserved, but it was broader and had almost the same weight as the longer horn (3 kg). Three independent drawings of the shorter horn are in existence.

The Gold Horns suffered a sad fate. In 1802, they were stolen from a royal cabinet by an impoverished goldsmith and forger, who smashed them and melted them down at once. They are now only known from drawings and measurements. Nevertheless, the Gold

Horns are an integral part of Danish national heritage. Almost every Dane has heard of them. They represent the treasures that can be found buried in Danish soil and are messages from a fantastic, mysterious and glorious past. Adam Oehlenschläger who wrote the Danish national anthem, also wrote a poem entitled *"The Gold Horns"* just after the horns were stolen. He describes the horns as being gifts from the Gods of Nature to those people,

Who perceive the High

In *Nature's Eye*

Later in the poem are the lines:

Then sounds in mould

The ancient gold

And yet people perceived the horns only for their curiosity and gold value. The Gods of Nature give up trying to enlighten those people, and the poem ends:

The truthful moment now has come,

The sacred gift forever gone.

Thankfully, we still have rather accurate drawings of this unique find, providing us with the opportunity of understanding the message of the horns. Indeed, the many symbols of the horns offer an explanation, in detail, for how the ancient Germanic peoples comprehended human life.

The use of drinking horns

There is no doubt that drinking horns were used in rituals by Germanic tribes. Almost all chieftains had two drinking horns buried in their graves alongside them. There is further testimony for this in the findings of mountings and chains made of silver or bronze, which were sometimes gilded. Julius Caesar in the first century BC wrote that the Germanic tribes hunted oxen or aurochs: *"Their horns differ very much from those of our oxen in size and shape, and kind. The Germani collect them eagerly, encase their edges in silver, and use them as beakers at their most magnificent banquets"*. The Roman author Plinius from the first century AD recorded that the Germanic people drank from auroch horns and that they always filled two horns.

The deities worshipped by drinking from the two horns were "the Divine Twins". They were, in many cases, depicted as two young men, but they sometimes appeared as two snakes, two dogs, two

Fig 2. The uppermost ring of the short horn; Drawing by Paulli

birds or two monsters. The Divine Twins can be seen in the decoration of almost all the silver mountings on Germanic drinking horns.

The Divine Twins appear several times on the Gold Horns. Figure 2 shows the decoration on the uppermost ring of the short horn. Here we see the Divine Twins represented by two horned gods on the convex side of the horn and by two warriors on the concave side.

The Sutton Hoo ship-burial is the richest archaeological discovery from the Germanic Era. It is the heathen funeral monument of Redwald, King of the East Angles (AD 615-628). Among the many precious grave gifts were his two drinking horns, which are of unusually large proportions. The silver mounting around the rim had several pairs of human masks, illustrating the Divine Twins. The terminals of the horns had silver mountings with bird-head finials, meaning that each horn contains the force of one of the Divine Twins. Similar horns were found in a rich burial in Taplow, Berkshire (figure 3).

Most of the treasures of the Sutton Hoo ship-burial have depictions of the Divine Twins. Figure 4 shows a replica of the magnificent helmet from the grave. The motive appears on some of the bronze plates on the helmet, as seen in the enlarged image beside the

3. Silver mounting of one of the two drinking horns from Taplow in Berk-shire

Fig 4. Replica of the helmet from the Sutton Hoo ship-burial

helmet. Here we see the Divine Twins performing a war-dance.

The worship of the Divine Twins was common to all Germanic tribes, and to many other peoples too such as the South American Indians, the Baltic peoples, the Greeks, the Romans and many more. It is a very old worldwide religion. The Divine Twins were believed to steer or direct the life of the individual. They could be present in many places in the outside world and inside a person. When the Divine Twins were invoked at a ritual, they were then present inside the participants of the drinking ritual, and when they drank from the horns, the Divine Twins also drank. In this way, the participants would feel the divine power of the Divine Twins inside of themselves.

Drinking horns were particularly used at the midwinter festival. The Divine Twins were involved in the continuation of life and the new cycle of life that began at midwinter. Medieval calendar sticks were marked with the horn as a symbol for midwinter and New Year. In medieval guilds, participants drank from the same horn in order of precedence. A similar procedure probably took place during Germanic drinking rituals.

Figure 5 shows a wall painting from Pompeii, destroyed by volcanic eruption by AD 78. Here, we see a Roman family worshipping the Divine Twins, and their mother. The Roman version of these deities were Castor, Pollux and Leda. Later in the book, we will address the picture of the Divine Twins on the short horn to see if we can

Fig 5. Wall painting from Pompeii

Runic Inscription

We know from the provenance of the horns that there is no grave, so the horns were not a grave gift. The burial of the two horns some distance apart, but near the surface also suggests that a treasure stash is unlikely. Consequently, we could presume that the burial of the horns was as a sacrifice. The name of the village, Gallehus means "house at the gallows", meaning that Gallehus, in ancient times, was a place where the gods could be contacted. It was a good place to make a sacrifice. As two drinking horns were used for worshipping the Divine Twins, I would assume that the sacrifice of the Gold Horns was dedicated to them.

The Divine Twins were able to guide and direct people, particularly when on a voyage. As far as we know, all migrating Germanic tribes worshipped the Divine Twins. The purpose of that worship was not

Fig 6. The Germanic runic alphabet in the outer circle and the sound of the runes in the inner circle

to be rewarded with a material output from the gods, but rather to demonstrate a trust in future life, hope, security, courage and energy. These values and effects were reinforced when the rituals were carried out in social groups. It is probable that the sacrifice of the horns was made on behalf of an entire tribe.

.

The short horn has a runic inscription at the rim (figure 2). This inscription may be able to explain why the horns were buried. The runes belong to the Germanic runic alphabet which contains 24 runes (figure 6).

The runic inscription says;

"EKHLEWAGASTICh HOLTIJACh HORNA TAWIDO"

This can be translated as: "I, guest of the living, from Holt, the horn I have done". Let us explore the inscription in more detail.

EKHLEWAGASTICh

"Lev" is a suffix of many Danish village names. The corresponding ending in England is "ley" and in Germany, "leben". In German "leute" means "living people". The person, named "Levgast", who sacrificed the Gold Horns must have been rich and powerful. I believe that the "Levgast" named here is also mentioned somewhere else. Almost the same name can be found in the *Nibelungenlied* [The Song of the Nibelungs], a heroic epic poem written in Middle High German. The Nibelungens were the Burgundian royal house. Together with a Sarmatian tribe and some East Germanic tribes, the Burgundies invaded the Roman Empire in AD 407, establishing a kingdom around Worms. The Roman army in northern France and Belgium was composed of Saxon and Scandinavian mercenaries. After a few years, they attacked the Burgundies around the year AD 415. According to the *Nibelungenlied*, a participant of the attack, Liudegast, was king of Denmark. The Burgundies killed twenty-nine Danish knights but Liudegast, being rich in gold, was captured and brought to Worms as a hostage. The Burgundies allowed one survivor to return to the Danish camp with the news of their king's capture. After a few years, Liudegast agreed to be a vassal of the Burgundies and was released. In AD 436, the Burgundian king attempted a military campaign in Belgium, but here the Burgundies were completely defeated by Romans, Saxons and Huns.

We may assume that Levgast returned to southern Jutland around the year AD 420 and organised a migration to England. Levgast was a professional warrior who had served in the Roman army. It was normal practice for young Germanic tribe leaders to serve in an army of a foreign king. Through military service abroad they received an education, wealth and fame. Tacitus writes about the Germanics:

If their native state sinks into the sloth of prolonged peace and repose, many of its noble youths voluntarily seek those tribes which are waging some war, both because inaction is odious to their race, and because they win renown more readily in the midst of peril, and cannot maintain a numerous following except by violence and war.

This description by Tacitus from AD 100 could be relevant for the tribes in southern Jutland around AD 400. From his contact with other Saxon warriors, Levgast probably had good knowledge of the situation in Britain around AD 420 and may well have known in which area to settle.

HOLTIJACh

Levgast says that he comes from Holt, which must have been a familiar place for both the people and the gods who lived in the area around Gallehus. The nearest place with the name of Holt is a village 25 km from Gallehus (figure 7).

HORNA TAWIDO

Most experts are of the opinion that the expression "I have done" refers to the manufacture of the horn. But since Germanic craftsmen do not normally mention their names, it is more likely that the expression refers to the burying of the horn. The entire inscription is aimed at the gods. Perhaps Levgast was the owner of the horn? The inscription refers to the sacrifice of the horn and what Levgast "[has] done" in Gallehus is the sacrifice. The word TAWIDO was written in very thin runes, possibly in connection with the burying of the horn.

It would not have been appropriate for the valuable horn to be sacrificed privately, i.e., for the chieftain alone. When a chieftain made such a sacrifice, he was showing his confidence in the tribal gods and the tribe would have confidence in him as the leader of the migration. So we can assume that the sacrifice was on behalf of an entire tribe. Only an important event for the tribe would require such a precious gift to the gods and that event could have been a considerable part of the tribe migrating. On April 16th AD 413, there was a total solar eclipse in southern Jutland. This very rare and dramatic event could indeed have given rise to the migration and the sacrifice of the horns.

The Migration of the Angles

The Venerable Bede recorded:

> From the Angles, that is, the country which is called Anglia, and which is said, from that time, to remain desert to this day, between the provinces of the Jutes and the Saxons, are descended the East Angles, the Midland Angles, Mercians, all the race of the Northumbrians, that is, of those nations that dwell on the north side of the river Humber, and the other nations of the English.

Archaeological finds document that people from Jutland and northern Germany migrated to England after AD 400. In fact, there is a remarkable decrease in the population of southern Jutland in the middle of the AD 400s. The migrants were not whole tribes but smaller ethnic groups of less than 100 people. These migrations carried on for about 150 years. Bede places an old homeland of the Angles between the Jutes and the Saxons. But there were several tribes and ethnic groups in southern Jutland and we cannot be certain that one of them was called Anglian. When these people migrated to England they were all called Angles. Bede called the Germanic population in England *gens angelorum*, under which he included the Jutes and the Saxons, because, in his eyes, all the Germanic invaders had the same cultural background. They worshipped the same god, Ing, one of the Divine Twins. The name Angles means "Ing's descendants" or "Ing's supporters". Noah Webster, the American lexicographer, speculated as early as 1823 that Ing gave his name to England. According to Bede, the Angles settled in all of England north of the Thames. The Saxons settled south of the Thames and the Jutes settled in Kent and on the Isle of Wight.

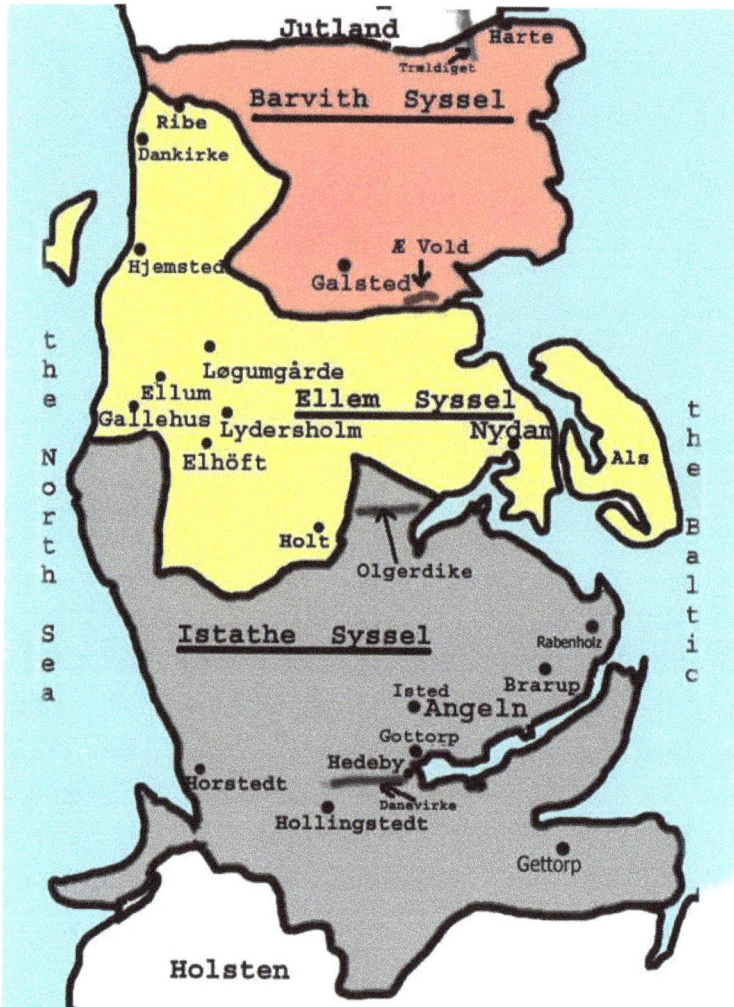

Map labels:

Jutland
Harte
Trældiget
Barvith Syssel
Ribe
Dankirke
Æ Vold
Hjemsted
Galsted
Løgumgårde
Ellum
Ellem Syssel
Gallehus
Lydersholm
Nydam
Elhöft
Als
Holt
Olgerdike
Istathe Syssel
Rabenholz
Isted
Brarup
Angeln
Gottorp
Hedeby
Horstedt
Danevirke
Hollingstedt
Gettorp
Holsten

the North Sea

the Baltic

7. *Three syssels in southern Jutland that were once the homeland of the Angles*

It is possible that we can trace the emigrants from southern Jutland with the help of old place names. The oldest subdivision of Jutland was into "syssels'", which were probably named after ancient tribes. Figure 7 shows the three southernmost syssels in Jutland. In the Late Middle Ages (AD 1375), these syssels were formed into the Duchy of Slesvig. However, today Barvith Syssel and most of Ellem Syssel is part of Denmark while Istathe Syssel is part of Germany.

The chapters that follow describe the emigration from these three syssels beginning with Ellem Syssel, the origin of the first organised emigration. But first the question of why theses peoples migrated needs to be addressed.

In the period of the great migrations (AD 375-575), the world temperature was 0.4 degrees Celsius lower than in the preceding and following periods. This may have caused a reduction in food, thus forcing the conquest of new areas for exploitation, and this may have been a catalyst for the Germanic migrations. The North Sea *had a nasty little jump in level between AD 350 and 550, flooding the coasts of northern Europe with an extra 2 feet of water. At the start of this rise, the areas along the North Sea cost were well -settled. Then the sea level rose, sending the inhabitants, Angles, Frisians and Saxons fleeing into ill-prepared Roman territories.* The Germanics were not very bound to their settlements; younger generations owned neither houses nor livestock. Rather houses were constructed of wood with every generation building new ones in new places. They had no fortifications and no king to protect their home. Protection was found within the tribe.

Southern Jutland was inhabited by at least three militant tribes who settled there as early as in Roman times. The Romans exploited the Germanics for slaves and as mercenaries, and the Germanic tribes also fought each other. Undoubtedly, southern Jutland, protected by sea and forests, seemed like an attractive place given these harsh conditions. But tribes fought each other here, too, as is witnessed by the barricades, sacrifices of war booty and legends. At the southern border of Barwith Syssel, the remains of a palisade called "Æ vold" dated to AD 279 have been found (figure 7). A ditch was dug south of the palisade, indicting a need for defence against enemies coming from the south. At the northern border of Istathe Syssel was the Olgerdike (figure 7), which guarded against enemies coming from the north. Three rows of palisades were found in this dike, dating to AD 123, 140 and 201, respectively.

After AD 400, the situation for the tribes in southern Jutland became more difficult owing to the military pressure from Danish kings coming from the Danish islands. The Germanics would neither be controlled by foreigners nor go to war for them. Moreover, there were internal wars of succession – many reports of unsuccessful successors having to flee for their life exist. Fights over kingship were normal whenever a king died. But even for small landowners, the order of succession could be reason enough to emigrate because the tradition in a Germanic family was for there to be only one heir. Indeed, all the reasons for the Germanic migration can be summarised as one: they were a people with a strong need for freedom. A freedom which could be achieved in Britain, where there were no rulers once the Romans had dissipated.

The Danes, on the other hand, were not a tribe, but rather an alliance of chieftain families. Any small king or chieftain could be called a Dane if he accepted being part of the alliance and remained loyal to the Danish "high" king. We know that the Danish kings visited each other and carried out religious rituals such as the drinking horn ritual together. It is worth noting that the Danish kings did not necessarily have familial relations to each other. This social system differed from a tribal society, wherein the king was ethnically related to his people. The word "king" derives from "kin relationship". The Danish groups were obliged to help the Danish high king in war. They were not free. But this alliance gave the Danes both a certain guarantee that they would not be attacked by other Danes and the strength to defeat non-Danish tribes.

The word "Dane" comes from the Indo-European stem *dan* meaning "floating". For instance, the Greeks in Homer's epic poem the *Illiad* were called Danaen. And the great rivers in Eastern Europe have names like Danube and Don. The first time we hear about Danes in Scandinavia is around AD 275 when the Greek Aikthikos travelled around the Baltic Sea. He met Danes, whom he says were the best shipbuilders and seafarers (Wüttke, 1853).

Furthermore, textual evidence offers a better understanding of the situation in southern Scandinavia around AD 500, specifically *the Beowulf Poem*, regarded as the most important work of old Anglo-Saxon literature. Sam Newton has indicated how the poem originated (Newton 1993). The small Anglo-Saxon kingdoms in England in the AD 500s already had a warrior elite. In the royal mead halls, they listen to poems celebrating heroes from the past, sometimes with accompaniment from a lyre. These poems described the warrior class's ideals: strength, agility, cruelty, loyalty, adornment, weapons and lineage. The deeds of the kings' ancestors and the royal pedigree were kept alive for generations, in particular. Indeed, this oral literature established an ideal self-image for the aristocracy and excluded anyone who did not live up to those standards. The heroic past was so essential to the identity of the rulers that the poems even survived into Christian times. Only Christian monks could write, but the bishops and monks belonged to the establishment of the ruling families. The first written versions of *Beowulf* were probably composed in a monastery in East Anglia in first half of the AD 700s. The version we know today was probably transcribed in the AD 1000s.

In its 3182 lines, *Beowulf* provides us with an excellent description of the situation around AD 500 in southern Scandinavia where the Danes dominated. The first 11 lines describe the Danish king Scyld, who probably lived around AD 450 (Translation by Slade, 2002).
Listen! We...of the Spear-Danes
In the days of yore, of those clan-kings;

Heard of their glory.
How those nobles performed courageous deeds.
Often Scyld, Scef's son...from enemy hosts,
From many peoples, seized mead-benches;
And terrorised the fearsome Heruli
After first he was found helpless and destitute,
He then knew recompense for that:
He waxed under the clouds, throve in honours,
Until to him each of the bordering tribes
Beyond the whale-road had to submit
And yield tribute; that was a good king!

The king's name "Scyld" means "guilt" or "debt", probably referring to the tributes he received. His descendants were called Scyldings. *Beowulf* mentions several other Danish chief clans but the Scyldings were the most powerful of them. It is not clear from the poem where the Scyldings had their home, but it was very likely on Funen, near Gudme ("the home of God"). The archaeological finds from the great settlement in Gudme are exceptional. In the AD 400s, the area of south-eastern Funen was home to one of the richest societies in northern Europe with more than fifty contemporaneous houses and several cemeteries. The wealth in gold must have come from tributes and participation in wars.

In line 6, we hear that the "Heruli" have been terrorised by the Danes. In the original old English text the word is "Eorle". The word "Eorl" is the same as the word "Eril" found in runic inscriptions from around AD 500 on. *Eril* was a title of the chief of the tribe, meaning spokesman (from "oral"). The Romans called some tribes of Scandinavian origin "Heruli" because they were led by an Eril. Sometime later, *Eril* became "jarl" in Scandinavia and "earl" in England. Some of the "Heruli" mentioned in line 6 are probably groups from southern Jutland who would later migrate to England.

Ellem Syssel

The old English poem *Widsith* tells us about tribes in the AD 400s. For example:

> Offa ruled Anglen, Alewih the Danes, who was the most spirited of all those people; he did not, however, accomplish heroic achievements beyond those of Offa, for of these men Offa, being in his youth, first conquered the greatest of kingdoms. No one contemporary with him made a greater heroic achievement in battle. With his lone sword he defined a frontier against the Myrgingas at Fifeldor.

Fifeldor is the mouths of River Eider at the southern border of Istathe Syssel. The Danes must have been neighbours to the north of the Angles. The name of their ruler, Alewih, probably stems from *al,* "grow, crop", and *awi,* "island". An island in Ellem Syssel a little north of Old Anglen has the name Als, also meaning "grower island". According to Old Norse legends, king Eylime (probably from Ellem Syssel) had a daughter, who had a son Sigurd, known as "Siegfried the Dragonslayer" in the *Nibelungenlied.* Sigurd's father was killed and his mother then married the Danish king Alv, thereby giving the Danes influence in Ellem Syssel. Alv lived around AD 400 and Alewih, around AD 450 when Offa was "in his youth", but they may have belonged to the same royal house as their names began with an "A". It seems that the Danish group of chieftains from eastern Denmark had installed a ruler in part of Ellem Syssel, namely the island of Als.

Sigurd fought for the Burgundies in the war against the Saxons around AD 415, and married the daughter of the Burgundian king. Levgast fought for the Saxons and was taken prisoner by the Burgundians, making Levgast and Sigurd old enemies. Sigurd was allied to the Danes, and his family had a claim to the throne of Ellem

Syssel, which may be the reason for the migration of Levgast from Ellem Syssel. The Ellem tribe was the first in southern Jutland to be threatened by the Danes and the first ones to emigrate.

What is more notable is that Gallehus, where the Gold Horns were buried, lies in Ellem Syssel, where we also have the village Ellum (figure 7). Ellum means "elle home", but the meaning of "elle" is questionable. Personally, I believe it meant "mighty" or "vigorous", which would be an appropriate name for the tribe. The word *el*ephant means "mighty phantom". *El*ves are powerful spirits. The Scandinavian word "elv" is a vigorous river. Elle was a common personal name during this time in history. According to the Anglo Saxon Chronicle, a chieftain named Elle came to the land of Britain with 3 ships in AD 477, landing near Southampton. He ruled in Sussex from AD 477 to 515. Moreover, near Southampton is Eling, formerly Elinges ("followers of Elle"). Aelle was also the name of the king of the Anglian kingdom Deira from AD 560 to 589.

Place names similar to the place names of Ellem Syssel are found in only one area of England: an area north of Norwich in Norfolk. Here, we have Aylsham, Eylmerton, North Elmham and South Elmham all called after Ellem. In North Elmham was found Spong Hill, the greatest cemetery in England from the Anglo Saxon time with 2259 cremation burials from the period AD 450 to 600, each covered with a small barrow.

Another place name peculiar to the same area north of Norwich is Reepham probably named after Ribe in Ellem Syssel. Horstead, in the same area, is probably named after Horstedt in Istathe Syssel. Ludham, northeast of Norwich, could be named after either Lydersholm or Løgumgårde in Ellem Syssel. Most remarkable is the village of Holt in the area north of Norwich. The name Holt can only be found in one place in Jutland, namely in Ellem Syssel – the very

Holt mentioned in the runic inscription on the short horn.

The emigration from Ellem Syssel was one of the first systematised emigrations of Angles to Britain that we know of. The journey was organised by family groups. Germanic people would not have felt safe abroad without their kinsmen. The similarity of place names highlights that the settlement was structured around groups who came from the same locality.

Norfolk already had a special place in history even before the Germanic invasion as it was home to the British Iceni tribe and did not became a colony like most of the Roman province of Britain. Prasutagus, ruler of the Iceni tribe who had ruled as a nominally independent ally of Rome, left his kingdom jointly to his daughters and the Roman Emperor in his will. However, when he died, his will was ignored — the kingdom was annexed as if conquered by the Romans, Prasutagus' widow, Queen Boudica, was flogged and her daughters raped as a statement of enslavement. In AD 60, while the Roman governor, Suetonius, was leading a campaign in northern Wales, Boudica led the Iceni people, along with the Trinovantes and some others, in revolt. They destroyed Camulodunum (modern-day Colchester), formerly the capital of the Trinovantes. Londinium (London) was burnt to the ground, as was Verulamium (St Albans). An estimated 70,000–80,000 people were killed in the three cities. Suetonius, meanwhile, regrouped his forces and, despite being heavily outnumbered, defeated the Britons in the Battle of Watling Street. The crisis caused Emperor Nero to consider withdrawing all Roman forces from Britain, but Suetonius' eventual victory over Boudica re-secured Roman control over the province. Boudica then killed herself to avoid capture. The Iceni were killed or escaped to wetlands. Tacitus described the defeat of the Iceni, writing "Rome creates a desert and call it peace", and in the years that followed, Norfolk had only a small population.

Archaeological finds of cremation burials show that some Germanics lived in Roman Britain as early as the AD 300s. Some may have been discharged Roman soldiers that came from Germanic populations within the Roman Empire. Some scholars (Myres, 1986) believe that these settlers were *laeti*. *Laeti* was a term, used in the late Roman Empire, to denote communities of people from outside the Empire who were granted land and permitted to settle on imperial territory on the condition that they provided recruits for the Roman military. *Laeti* were in use during the AD 200s and AD 300s and almost all of them were Germanics. In Britain, they tended to settle near the

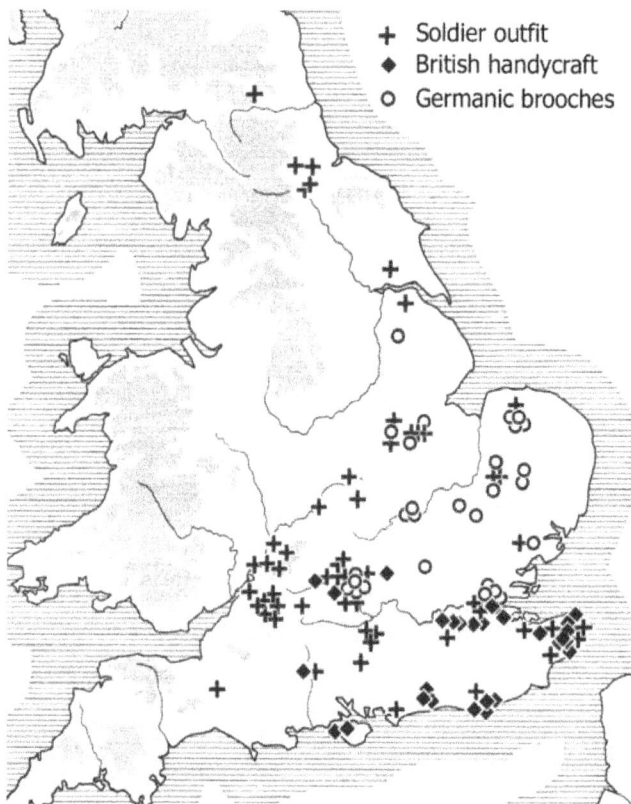

Fig 8. Finds from the first half of the AD 400s (Böhme 1986)

Roman fortresses.

In AD 407, the Roman military in Britain chose as their leader Constantine III, named after the famed emperor of the early AD 300s Constantine the Great, who himself had risen to power through a military coup in Britain. In order to seize power as Roman emperor, Constantine III left Britain with the Roman troops. The Britons then revolted against the Roman administrators by taking up arms and defending the towns against the Barbarians. Power was seized by smaller kings. However, this process did not succeed north of the Thames, probably because the British population there was fewer and there were more Germanic *laeti*. East Anglia and the Middle lands were open for settlers.

According to Böhme (1986), Germanic troops stationed in Britain in the late AD 300s were transferred from garrisons on the Danube frontier and in Gaul. Military equipment, as illustrated in figure 8, from these troops, dating to the AD mid-400s has been found: soldier outfits are found throughout England, but very few in East Anglia; "British handicraft" refers to metal objects with ornaments in Romano-British style. In figure 8, we can see that British objects have been found in the same areas as the soldier outfits, probably because they belonged to the soldiers and their families; and Germanic brooches, dating to the first half of the AD 400s, are also noted in figure 8. The provenance of these cruciform brooches is Slesvig-Holstein, Germany, and they are considered Anglian. The brooches were used by women and signified the first non-military Anglian settlements. Figure 8 shows they have been found in East Anglia and in the upper Thames Valley (Oxfordshire). The settlements were accompanied by cemeteries, which had cremation burials. New cemeteries from the mid-400s AD indicate arrivals of new contingents from the North Sea coastal areas had settled in the Midlands and outside the original settlement area of East Anglia.

In Norfolk flows the river Wensum. This river is one of the few rivers in Britain with a Germanic name. *Wen* or *Wend* means "winding" and this river really does meander. The suffix *–sum* is common in Friesland and southern Jutland and means "a place". The Wensum River flows through Norwich, later becoming a tributary of the smaller River Yare. These rivers are and were navigable from Yarmouth up to Norwich. Moreover, it is possible that Norwich got its name from the god Njord/Nor, meaning "Njord's harbour". It is probable that the emigrants from Ellem arrived via this route.

I would estimate that a migration of this nature involved three boats at most. The boats used for the Germanic emigrations to England were rowing boats of the Nydam boat-type, from AD 350, found in Nydam Moor in southern Jutland. It was made of oak and was 23m long. Nydam Moor was the sacred site where the Ellem tribe deposited their war loots (figure 7).

In the fore of the Nydam boat two male figure heads were found (figure 9). The heads were designed to be removed from the boat and should probably be seen as idols, suggesting that the people

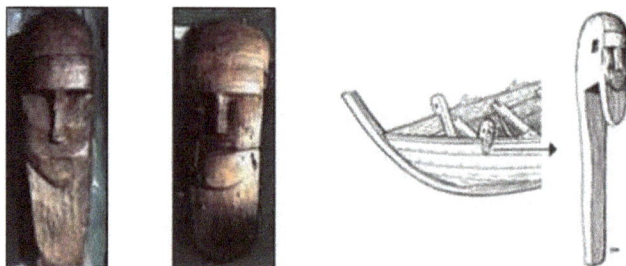

Fig 9. Two wooden heads from the front end of the Nydam boat (AD 350)

who sailed on the boat from the Baltic Sea had the Divine Twins with them, guiding them on their voyage.

The Nydam boat had room for 24 oarsmen and a number of passengers. At most, they could travel 30 km a day, so those on board would likely have gone ashore at night. The distance along the Frisian coast to Calais and, from there to Britain, is 1000 km. That would take roughly 33 days in good weather. In fact, many of the Germanic emigrants settled in Friesland, some even for years. This is verified by settlements from the AD 400s, found in the coastal areas of the North Sea.

The settlement of Hjemsted (figure 7), in Ellem Syssel, from around AD 450 has been excavated and a reconstruction can be seen in figure 10. This area was rich and flourished in the period AD 300 to 500. Many remains of iron production were found here. It is remarkable that the place name Hempstead is found in only four places in Britain, two of them being in Norfolk near the other place names that seem to have originated in Ellem Syssel. Perhaps

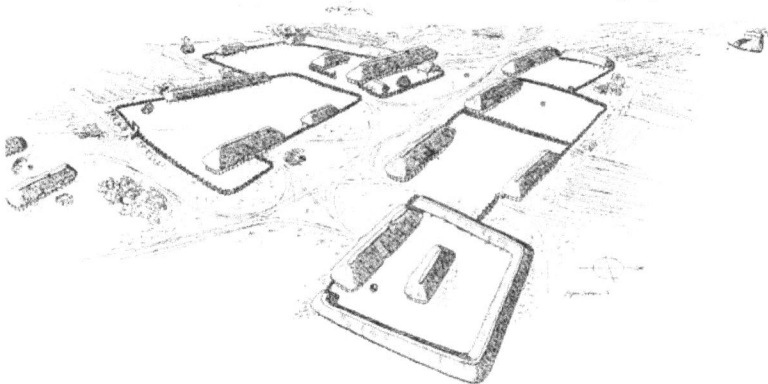

10. Reconstruction of the village of Hjemsted around AD 450

inhabitants of Hjemsted migrated to England in AD 450 and settled in Norfolk?

The archaeological finds from Germanic settlements in Jutland and the Anglo-Germanic settlements in England indicate that the communities were made up of a few farmsteads like those in Hjemsted or perhaps even smaller. Overall, the archaeological and skeletal evidence seems to point to the households forming the basic residential and economic units of society. The household comprised of 5-9 individuals, most likely the family of the master of the household and 3-4 children. We may add the odd unmarried brother, sister or surviving parent. The inhabitants of the community were ethnically and culturally related: for instance, men able to carry weapons came from the communities within a tribal area to meet at a *Thing*. And a powerful or clever household master was an *Eril* or earl, a "spokesman" of the Thing.

Istathe Syssel

In Istathe Syssel, we find the village Isted (figure 7) that once had a local court. The names *Istathe* and *Isted* are related to the Goddess of forth-bringing known as Easter, Eostra and Ostara. She was an aspect of the Mother of Life which is discussed in a later chapter. She was most popular among the tribes in southern Jutland and with the Angles in Britain. Istathe Syssel had a rather dense population. The tribe in the eastern part was the dominant one, economically and militarily-speaking, in some periods. I refer to this as Old Anglen. Indeed, the area of Istathe Syssel north of the Schlei is still called Anglen (figure 7). These Old Angles had a sacred place, Torsbjerg Moor, where they sacrificed their war loot. A nearby village is Süderbrarup, whose name relates to the word *bravo* and the Danish word *brage* meaning to talk loudly and make noise. Undoubtedly, referring to the Angels in Brarup having loud religious rituals. In the 5th century, when many Angles had emigrated, the sacrifices in Torsbjerg Moor came to an end.

Istathe Syssel had a dense population before the migration, which can be seen from both the many archaeological finds and pollen from useful plants preserved in the moors. Both were remarkably reduced at the end of the migration period. More or less the same phenomenon is seen in the rest of southern Jutland and in Holstein. Much can be gleaned about the Migration Era from the excavated burial sites. The activities in the cemeteries ended around AD 500 in Slesvig, Holstein, West Mecklemburg and the Elbe-Weser Area due to a substantial emigration (Böhme 1986).

The cemetery in Süderbrarup existed from around AD 150, when the Angle tribe arrived and was no longer in use around AD 575, when the migration period ended. 1234 burials were found; almost all of them were cremations in urns. Spong Hill, in Norfolk and mentioned earlier, is a similar site. There are precise parallels between the pottery forms and decoration of Süderbrarup and Spong Hill. A substantial part of the population in Istathe Syssel must have migrated to England.

However, there are cemeteries (Issendorf and Westerwanna) in the coastal area between the Rivers Elben and Weser that have the same parallels as Süderbrarup and Spong Hill. Issendorf was in use in the period AD 380-550 and has 5500 urn burials. This cemetery does not seem to have been introduced by the previous local population. Thus, it must have been used by the immigrants. Similar preliminary settlements from the AD 400s have been found along the North Sea coast in the Frisian area. The Frisian terp at Ezinge was abandoned in the AD 300s. In the AD 400s, new houses were build. Anglian pottery and cruciform brooches were also introduced, testifying to the lengthy stay – indeed, probably spanning years – of the many emigrants from southern Jutland at the North Sea coast before the crossing to England.

The history of the people of the North Sea coast is poorly understood. Those who desired contact with the Romans and later, the Francs, had to travel along the coast, and from there onto the Rivers Elbe and Rhine. Trade followed the same routes as slaves, weapons, hides, wool, cattle, fish, jewellery and money. There must have been a lot of shipping along the coast. According to the Romans, transportation by land was 60 times more expensive than transportation by sea. Moreover, those living by the sea had to adapt to the forces of nature. They had to be independent, inventive and brave. There are stories from the AD 300s of warrior groups from these areas, called Saxons, plundering the French and British coasts. The people at the North Sea coast were seafarers, who knew how to navigate the safe sailing routes. They were ready to migrate or to help other emigrants in return for payment. Around AD 400, wars between the tribes in southern Jutland break out. The ethnic groups in the western part, the marshland, were probably more in favour of emigration than partaking in these wars. They may have been the first Angles to emigrate, despite us not hearing about them.

In Anglen, there were three large cemeteries: Süderbrarup, Sörup and Husby. Süderbrarup is exceptional because the number of interments continued to increase, whereas the number of internments at the other two was already declining from AD 320, indicating that the majority of the population of Istathe Syssel had emigrated around AD 500 with the exception of the centre of power near Süderbrarup.

The first dated mention of Angles in Britain is AD 443, when *The Anglo-Saxon Chronicle* states that: "the Britons sent men to the chieftains of the Angles and asked for help against the Picts". We can assume that Offa was ruling the Angles in Istathe Syssel around AD 450 – the time of the migration of the Angles. Many of those Angles came to settle in Mercia. Note the sequence of kings of the Royal house of Mercia kings:

Wearmud – Offa – Angeltheow – Eomer – Icel – Cnebba – Cynevald – Creoda.

Creoda was the 6th king after Offa and is said to have ruled Mercia from AD 582. Thus, Offa could have been king around AD 450 – allowing 20 years for each generation.

The three first names on the list: Wearmud, Offa and Angeltheow, must have been kings in Istathe Syssel, the old homeland of the Angles.

The name Wearmud is comprised of *ver*, meaning "man" and *mundr*, meaning "protection". This name may refer to the Divine Twin of the name *Hermund,* meaning "high protector".

The name Offa is probably related to "offense", deriving from *of* and meaning "against" and *fend*, meaning "strike".

Angeltheow means "minister of Anglen"; *Theow* means "servant" or "minister" (the Latin word *minister* means "servant").

We do not know if Icel belonged to the lineage. The name *Icel* is probably derived from the British tribe, the Iceni, who lived in East Anglia before being massacred by the Romans. In the AD 500s, there was an ethnic group, known as the Iclingas, in the Midlands.

The story of *Beowulf* takes place around AD 515, when the young warrior, Beowulf, visits the Danish king Hrothgar, grandson of the aforementioned Danish king Scyld. Later Beowulf visits the hall in Old Anglen that once belonged to Offa. Here, Beowulf praises the heroic but now deceased king Offa, saying (line 1960) that Eomer was born in Offa's house. Beowulf also mentions that Eomer was a descendant of Offa's father, Garmund (Wearmud in the Mercia lineage), but a homage to Offa. This indicates that Offa was Eomer's grandfather. Eomer's mother was Offa's daughter. In other words, the line of the Royal house of Mercia was intact: Eomer was successor and possibly son of Angeltheow, who, in turn, was married to Offa's daughter.

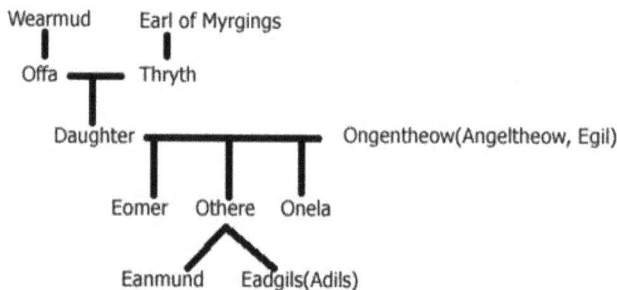

Fig 11. Descendants of Wearmud and Ongentheow

The old English *Widsith* poem is probably the oldest known poem in a Germanic language and it provides a very reliable catalogue of Germanic heroes, tribes and places around AD 500. According to *Widsith*, Ongentheow was king of Sveer. Ongentheow is also mentioned several times in *Beowulf*. Ongentheow is the same person as Angeltheow. The slight difference in the names could be due to the different languages. In the writings of Snorri Sturluson, the Swedish king Egil has the same two sons that Ongentheow has in *Beowulf*, namely Othere and Onela. So we can assume that Ongentheow and Egil were the same person. The cremated remains of Egil/Ongentheow were found in a grave mound in Uppsala, Sweden, dating to AD 510-15.

It is notable that the name Eomer begins with a vowel akin to the other members of the Swedish royal family. The reason for that this is the belief that the Swedish kings descended from the god Ing and were called Ynglinger. Angeltheow and Offa's daughter had two other sons together, Othere and Onela, and their names also start with a vowel (figure 11).

The solution to the problem of the origin of King Ongentheow could be that he was born in Sweden but came to King Offa in Old Anglen as a mercenary. It was normal for a young prince to join the hird of a powerful king in the hope that it would educate the prince as a warrior, and bring him fame and wealth. Beowulf did the same when he visited the Danish king Hrothgar. Ongentheow probably did marry King Offa's daughter. Offa died sometime around AD 480. His grandson, Eomer, migrated to England and became the first king of Mercia.

Offa's daughter became the ruling queen of Old Anglen around AD 480-500, and her husband, with the name Ongentheow ("minister of Anglen"), became the military ruler. In time, Ongentheow also inherited the Swedish kingdom and here he was the ruling king, residing there for the majority of the time, whereas Offa's daughter resided in Old Anglen.

The map in figure 12 shows that the Germanic immigrants settled near rivers. They sailed up rivers in rowing boats until they found fertile soil. They avoided large forests and the wet areas near marshes. It is interesting that they also avoided Roman remains:

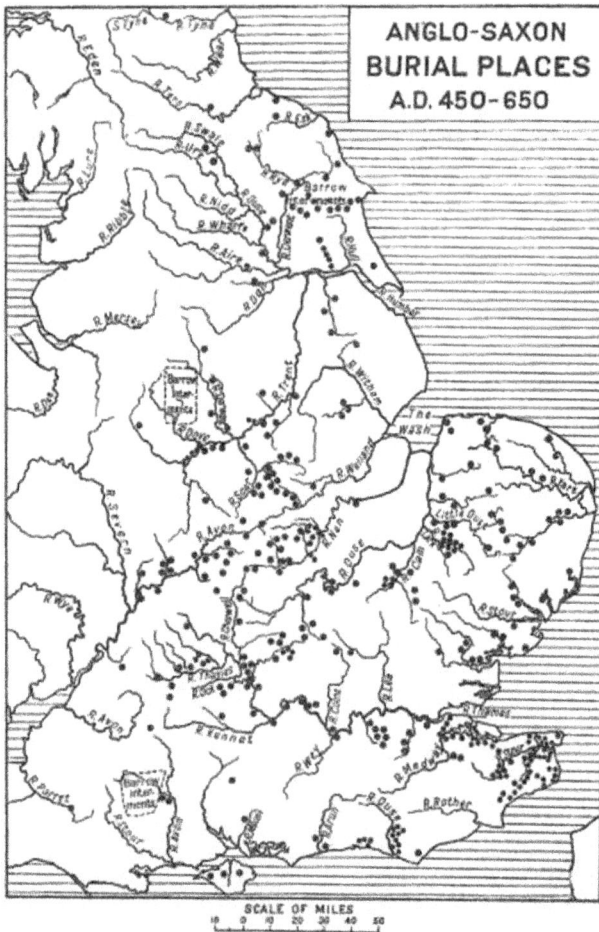

12. Anglo-Saxon burial sites (Leeds 1970)

roads, towns and farms. The Britons preferred to live in stone houses in towns but the Germanics built houses of wood. Only in Kent was there found a number of Germanic cemeteries near Roman settlements. This may be attributed to the peculiar origin of the Kentish settlers.

The immigration of Germanics into England took off around AD 450. At this time, the Roman military presence was finally coming to an end, probably because there were no transfers of new troops from the continent. The archaeological finds from the soldier-outfits (figure 8) also cease around AD 450. Following this the British commanders asked for help from the Angles as there had been a substantial immigration of Angles from Istathe Syssel and from other areas by the North Sea Coast. They settled in East Anglia, in the Midlands and by the Thames river-bed.

The first immigrants in Mercia settled along the River Trent. They arrived by sea, via the River Humber and from there, via the River Trent. The marshy land on its lower reaches was uninhabitable and as in the Fens, the Angles penetrated right into the interior of the country before finding a place to settle. Eomer may have followed the same route. The name Trent is thought to be a Roman name or perhaps a Celtic name, but I believe the Angles may have used it due to its similarity to *Trene*, the greatest river in Isthate Syssel. When a spring tide meets the downstream of Trent there is considerable tidal bore still referred to as "Trent Aegir". Aegir is the Angle name of the God of the Sea. Mercia became a strong, independent kingdom and was the last Anglo-Saxon kingdom to be Christianised.

The long River Eider forms the border between Slesvig and Holstein. The name *Eider* or *Aegidore* means "Aegir's door" and Aegir, God of the sea, is a terrifying Giant. Incidentally, the same name occurs in the Aegean Sea in Greece.

Saxo Grammaticus in his *Deeds of the Danes* tells us that Uffe (Offa, king of Angles) fought the Saxon's and defended the border against them, too. He writes that Offa won a single-combat held on an island in the middle of Eider, probably the island where Rendsborg Castle was later built. Saxo also tells us that "Wermund got for his son Uffe a wife, the daughter of Frowin, the earl of the men of Slesvig. Then the Swedish king Atisle (Eadgils) attacked and killed Frowin". Moreover, "Frowin's sons, Ket and Wig, went to Sweden in disguise and assassinated Atisle (Eadgils)". The killing of Frowin could have happened when Eadgil was exiled from the Geats in Istathe Syssel ca. AD 530. Saxo's statement is obviously wrong since Offa died around AD 480. The historian Saxo very often places old historic events in the wrong sequence. Nevertheless, it is quite possible that Offa married the princess of the tribe that he had besieged. *Beowulf* tells us that Offa's bride, Thryth, came to him over the water, probably the River Eider.

According to *Widsith*, Offa's victorious sword fight was against the Myrginger ("moor walkers"). Frowin's family had their homeland in the swampy area south of the River Eider. In the royal house of Wessex, we find king Frowin and his son king Ket. Their old homeland, south of the Eider, was indeed close to the Saxon area. It is possible that Ket migrated around AD 540, becoming king in Wessex. He is one of several examples of the migration of defeated Anglian rulers from southern Jutland.

The Geats

Beowulf recounts Ongentheow fighting with the Geats – probably over power in Istathe Syssel. Beowulf did not belong to the Geat lineage, but he did grow up with the Geats. From *Beowulf* we learn that the Geats were West Danes. They were not a tribe but a family of chieftains called Geats/Goths. In such troubled times, it was a good solution for such a group of warriors to join the Danish kings.

The name *Geat* has generated many arguments over its provenance: Gotland, in the Baltic Sea, Östergötland, Vestergötland and Gotaland (a former name of Jutland) to name a few. All these words (including the tribal name "Goths") mean "good", and originally meant "fit, adequate, belonging together". The proto-Indo-European root *ghedh* means "to unite, be associated, suitable". Many Germanic groups would call themselves suitable in their own dialect. *Geat* was probably pronounced with j-sound. Interesting and noteworthy, regarding words meaning "good", is the use of the Old Norse word *gothi* to refer to a leader of the community during the Viking Age. In Old Gothic, the title was "gudja". This was common in Iceland, where there was no king. But the title "gothæ" is also found on runic stones in southern Scandinavia. The gothi was not a warrior but a religious, political and economic authority of the community: priest, decision maker and landowner.

Perhaps their homeland was in Istathe Syssel? Beowulf was nephew of the Geat King Hygelac, son of Hrethel (figure 13). We know from the records of Gregor of Tours that the "Danish King Hugleicus" was felled in a battle at the mouth of the Rhine in AD 520. Beowulf escaped from the battle and later became king of the Geats. In Istathe Syssel, we have the village Hollingstedt (figure 7) formerly known as Huglestad, probably meaning "Hygelac's town". Maybe the Geats had seized power in part of Istathe Syssel at this time, as some place names – for instance, Gettorf and Gottorp – could refer to the Geats/Goths (figure 7). There is, however, reason to believe that the Geats' original homeland was south of the Schlei, near Eckernförde Inlet, in modern-day Germany (figure 14) – in Beowulf's time at least. They might have moved there from somewhere in Scandinavia.

Around AD 500, the Swedish King's sons, Onela and Othere (in Swedish Ottar), attacked the Geats. In AD 505, Haethcyn, King of the Geats and his brother Hygelac attacked the Queen of Old Anglen, Offa's daughter and Ongentheow's wife, capturing her. That same year Ongentheow attacked the Geats, rescuing his wife. Ongentheow's attack is featured in *Beowulf* (lines 2922-25):

Nor aught expect I of peace and faith
From Swedish folk. 'Twas spread afar
How Ongentheow reft at Ravenswood
Haethcyn Hrethling of hope and life.

These fights were probably battles for the power in Istathe Syssel. It can be assumed that the Geats were the superior force in Istathe Syssel at this time, despite many of the inhabitants having left for

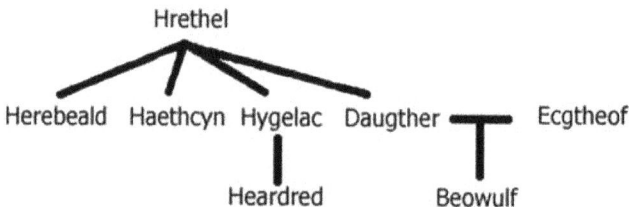

Hrethel

Herebeald Haethcyn Hygelac Daugther ⎯⎯ Ecgtheof

Heardred   Beowulf

13. Descendants of Hrethel and Ecgtheof

England. The nerve centre of the Angles was at Brarup, near Thorsberg Moor. Today, we find a nearby municipality called Rabenholz ("Ravenswood"). This is quite likely the site of the battle mentioned in *Beowulf*. Haethcyn, king of the Geats, was killed and his brother Hygelac succeeded him. During this attack Ongentheow was fatally injured, and brought to Sweden – presumably dead – to be buried in Uppsala. His son, Ohthere, subsequently became king of Sweden.

When Othere died ca. AD 530, his brother Onela took power. Othere's sons, Eadgils (in Swedish *Adils*) and Eanmund, had the right to the kingship and were threatened by Onela. They escaped to Geat land, where Hygelac's son Heardred was king. Onela then immediately attacked Geat land, killing his nephew Eanmund and King Heardred. He then returned to his home in Sweden, leaving Beowulf to hold the throne and rule the Geats. Five years later, however, Eadgils took his revenge, killing his uncle while invading Sweden with arms and men supplied by Beowulf, now king of Geat land. Subsequently, Eadgils became king of Sweden.

Lines 2939-44 tell us more about Ongentheow's attack on the Geats:

Then he besieged the huge (sacred) grove, the survivors of swords
Weary and wounded; he often threatened woes
To the wretched company in the length of the night
Said: he in the morning, by the edges of a maiche,
He would sacrifice one of them on the gallows-tree
As game for the birds.

Ongentheow belonged to the Swedish Yngling clan who believed they were descendants of the god Ing. His intention was to sacrifice the prisoner Haethcyn to Ing by hanging him from a gallows in the sacred grove of Ravenswood. But it never came to be, because Haethcyn was rescued by the Geats.

When the last king of the Geats, Beowulf, was dying, he had no descendants. In the last section of the poem are the lines:

From his neck Beowulf unclasped the collar of gold,
To his vassal he gave it.
"Thou art the remnant of all our race,
The Waegmunding name. For wyrd has swept
All my line to the land of doom."

Waegmunding means "member of the clan of Wearmud" (figure 11). It seems that a member of the old clan had survived during the Geatish rulership and could now once again assume power in Old Anglen.

The prominent archaeological find from Istathe Syssel at the time of the Geats is gold bracteates: thin, gold amulets, printed on only one side and used as pendants. About 1000 bracteates have been found. They were produced in the period AD 475-565 and most of them are found in southern Scandinavia. Often, the depictions on the gold bracteates are inspired by the portrayal of gods on Roman coins, but the gods on the gold bracteates are Germanic as we will see later and they provide further understanding of the beliefs among the elite, warrior class.

Karl Hauck has demonstrated that some types of gold bracteates were invented in Gudme on Funen (Hauck 1985-1989). Many bracteates have been found near Gudme and were obviously produced there. Presumably, the leading Danish king Hrothgar had his hall on Funen and the powerful Danish Royal family resided there. They possessed gold and invented the use of gold bracteates. When the Danish king gathered with other Danish chiefs to perform a ritual (doubtless an animal sacrifice or a drinking horn ritual), the gold bracteates were likely produced for the occasion and worn during the ritual. The participants' continual wearing of these pendants strengthened both the unity of the Danes and the loyalty between allies, despite them not belonging to the same ethnic group or family. Indeed, gold bracteates of lower quality were produced at the gatherings of minor rulers in southern Scandinavia.

When a gold bracteate is found in a grave and the sex of the interred can be identified it is almost always female. The woman of the house wore the gold bracteate. She was responsible for the house's provisions and supplies and she kept the gold. She was in charge of the drinking ritual. The welcome symbol on the long gold horn in figure 42 shows a woman offering a drink from a drinking horn. *Beowulf* develops further the picture of life in the mead hall.

Lines 612-17:
...Wealhtheow came forth
Hrothgar's queen, mindful of etiquette,
Greeted, gold-adorned, the men in the hall
And then the noble lady gave out full cups,
First to the East-Danes homeland-guardian
Bade him be blithe at the partaking of beer

Lines 622-25:
...Until the time came
That she to Beowulf, the ring-adorned queen
Blossoming in spirit, carried a mead-cup
She greeted the Geatish prince, thanked God

Wealhtheow means "power-servant", "minister of finance" and she wears plenty of gold adornments. The first cup is offered to the most powerful guest: the East Dane king, probably Hrothulf of Sealand. Later, she offers a cup to Beowulf, the offering being accompanied by thanking God. In another section of the poem, we are told that the queen gives Beowulf presents of gold – one of which was a gold neck ring. It is quite likely that he also received a gold bracteate. When Beowulf returns to the Court of the Geats he gives the neck ring to the Geatish queen.

It is obvious from the many finds of pairs of drinking horns that the worship of the Divine Twins via a drinking ritual was common to most Germanic tribes. *Beowulf,* the female graves and depictions such as those in figures 42 and 49 make it quite clear that the woman of the house was the leader of the ritual. For the Germanics, a woman had the best contact with the gods and the woman was in control of the gold. But it must be acknowledged that for the Germanics, gold was not a means of payment. Gold belonged to the gods and had divine power. Gold bracteates are found mostly as sacrificial hoards in many cases together with other gold articles.
Beowulf (lines 1684-86) says of the Danish King Hrothgar that he was "the finest of the world-kings between the seas who dealt out treasures on Scedenigge".

Scedenig is the original form of Scandinavia, most likely meaning "sheath waters". Danish *skede* means "sheath". The *Aw* of Scandin*avia* has the same origin as the Latin "aqua" and means "water". The greatest characteristic of south Scandinavia is its many narrow belts and sounds – or *sheaths*. In Beowulf's time "Danish" was the political designation of some rulers and *Scedenig* was the geographical designation of an area.

The distribution of gold bracteates in figure 14 shows that they were used and possibly produced south of the Schlei Inlet. Around AD 500 – the time in which they were in use – this area was probably controlled by the Geats. The introduction of the gold bracteates is attributed to the leading contemporary Danish king on Funen and they were certainly used by other kings of the Danish alliance. The

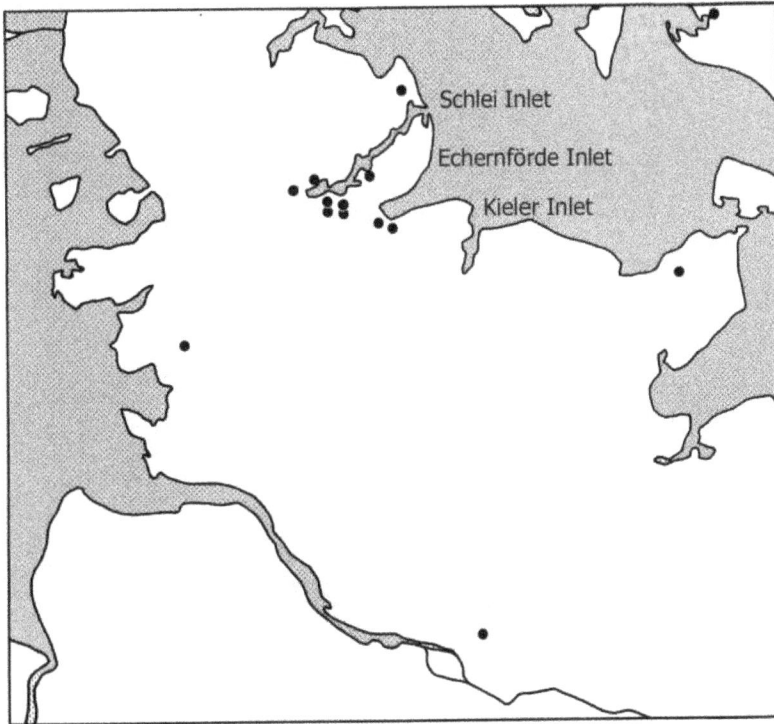

Fig 14. Gold bracteates found in Istathe Syssel and Holstein around AD 500

Geats were also Danish; hence, they probably produced gold bracteates themselves. Offa's daughter probably ruled the Angles, north of the Schlei, until around AD 500, though use of gold bracteates by her people is unlikely as they were not Danes.

Figure 15 shows one of the gold bracteates from the map in figure 13. The inscription in runes says:

A L G U   (meaning "I protect")

ALGU is possible related to both the Gothic word *alh* ("god, protector") and the name of the Germanic Divine Twins *Alki* ("protectors") as reported by Tacitus around AD 100. The ending "U" may be the first person singular. The protector must be the depicted deity. The swastika sign, left of centre, is a symbol for the turning of heaven, revealing that this god was in heaven. His enormous hair is

15. Gold bracteate from Geltorf by the Schlei (Hauck cat. 254)

a sign of his juvenile power while the bird in his hair depicts his ability to fly. Out of his mouth comes speech, because he gives advice. The eight balls are probably an illustration of the eight parts of night and day, which the Germanics allowed for (see later chapter).

There are good reasons to believe that Ing was the most popular god in southern Scandinavia, including among the Angles. He is depicted on most of the gold bracteates.

In *Beowulf*, the Danish king Hrothgar is called "the wise lord of the Ingwine" (line 1318) and "the protector of the Ingwine" (line 1043).

Ingwine means "friend of Ing", suggesting that Ing was worshipped by the people in southern Scandinavia. As early as AD 100, the Roman Tacitus called the Germanic people near the North Sea

Ingaevones and the Roman Plinius called them *Ingvaeones*. The Christian monks who recorded *Beowulf* tried to eliminate any pagan gods from the manuscript but sometimes it becomes apparent which god was worshipped around AD 500. Beowulf's sword is called *Incgelafe* (line 2577). The holy treasures of the Frisian king Finn are called *Incgegold* (line 1107), and line 1314 says "the ruler of the Elves could bring about a change for the better". The Elves are dead souls and it was told in Viking Mythology, that Frey (another name for Ing) had his home in Alfheim ("the home of Elves").

The Wulfings

The Wulfings were a militant ethnic group well known from many legends. When the Langobards lived in Holstein around AD 100, they are said to have had conflict with the Wulfings. The homeland of the Wulfings was probably in northern Holstein around the Kieler Inlet. Lines 28-29 of *Widsith* says:

Sigehere ruled the Sea-Danes for a long time,

Hnæf the Hocings, and Helm the Wulfings

The Wulfings are grouped with two Danish clans, indicating they were located in the same sphere. 30 km east of the Kieler Inlet we have the place name Helmstorf. According to legends, King Helm was killed and his son, Halga, and daughter, Wealhtheow, fostered by the Danish King Healfdene. Wealhtheow later married King Healfdene's son, Hrothgar, and she played a vital role at the court when Beowulf visited King Hrothgar around AD 515. Her name Wealhtheow implies a responsibility for both the finances and the delivering of treasures. Beowulf says: "Often twisted-rings she gave to the warriors". The heroic Halga, brother of Wealhtheow and foster-brother of Hrothgar, was dead at the time of Beowulf's visit. Halga's son, King Hrothulf was, however, present at the time. He was a Wulfing as his name indicates (figure 16). From the history of the

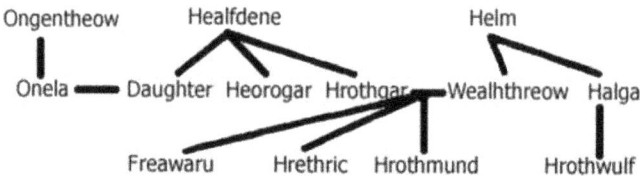

16. Descendants of Healfdene and Helm

Goths, we know that the Wulfing King Hrothulf carried out military service for Theodorich the Great (king of Goths AD 493-526), but by the time of Beowulf's visit in AD 515, King Hrothulf would have returned.

In *Beowulf* (lines 459-63), King Hrothgar speaks to Beowulf about his father Ecgtheow: "Your father kindled the greatest feuds among the Wulfings when he became the killer of Heatholaf. Because of fear of strife, Wulfingas was unable to keep him. Then he sought the South Danes over the surging waves".

Ecgtheof killed one of his own clan, the Wulfings, and fearing revenge, he asked the Danes for help. This was probably a good idea because the Danish Queen Wealhtheow was a Wulfing herself. Later, King Hrothgar (lines 470-72) says that he "sent ancient treasures over the waters to the Wulfings and made peace". The Wulfings and the Geats were neighbours. The name Ecgtheow means "edge servant, sword servant" and he had received this name because he was married to the Geat King Hredel's daughter and consequently not a true Geat. Ecgtheow's son, Beowulf, was both Geat and Wulfing, thus he received a name with "wulf". Beowulf was fostered by the Geats from the age of 7 when his father died. When Beowulf eventually became king of the Geats around AD 533, he probably soon came to hold the supreme power in Istathe Syssel.

Sam Newton has demonstrated that *Beowulf* was probably recited at the East Anglian royal court (Newton 1993). Beowulf was a Wulfing and the East Anglian kings were called Wulfings. Indeed, the descendants of the East Anglian Royal House have the following lineage:
Woden – Caser – Tyttman – Trygil – Hrotmund – Hryp – Wilhelm – Wehha – Wuffa – Tyttla - Redwald

Wehha is said to be the first king of East Anglia and he died in AD

571.

The name Wilhelm (later William) may be named after Helm, who ruled the Wulfings in the AD 400s. In *Beowulf*, Wulfings were also called Helmings. We find two contemporary Helminghams: one in Norfolk and one in Suffolk. Moreover, the town of Hemley is situated only four miles south of Sutton Hoe.

Caser means Roman Emperor. It is peculiar that he is only present in the East Anglian lineage. This may be due to Roman emperors claiming to descended from the twin wolfs Romulus and Remus.

The name Hrotmund appears in *Beowulf* as the son of Queen Wealhtheow and grandson of Helm (figure 16). Sam Newton has pointed out that Hrotmund possibly had to go into exile because of a dynastic struggle with his cousin Hrothulf over the Danish throne. Saxo writes in his *Legends* that Hrothulf (Rolf Krake) killed Hrethric

Fig 17. Gold bracteate from Undley, near Lakenheath in Suffolk, around AD 500

(Rorik), Hrothmund's brother (figure 16).

Despite being in agreement with almost all of Newton's arguments, evidence suggest the homeland of the Geats and the Wulfings was located on the south cost of the Baltic (figure 14) (see chapters "The Geats" and "The Wulfings").

A very interesting find from the Anglian settlers in England is a gold bracteate found in Undley near Lakenheath in Suffolk (figure 17). It was fitted with an eyelet and double spiral so it could be worn as an amulet. The inscription is one of the oldest of written English ever found. The runes have to be read from right to left, starting at the double spiral. They are all of the old Germanic type from figure 6 with the exception of the O-rune which is of Anglo-Frisian type. The three words are separated with a circle. The transcription in Latin letters is

GAGOGA MAGA MEDU

meaning "Yah Yoh Yah reward for kinsmen"

The three syllables of the first word are written as bind runes, with side-twigs attached to the X shape of the G-rune to represent the vowels A and O. The same word is found in an inscription on a lance -shaft sacrificed in the Kragehul Moor on Funen in the 5th century. Being an acclamation, it was probably pronounced "Yah Yoh Yah" (see figure 63).

MAGA means "kinsmen". Related to this is the Danish *mage* or "spouse".

MEDU means "reward". Related to the word *medal*. The suffix *-U* determines the dative case.

The inscription tells us that a leader gave copies of this medal to some of his kinsmen probably in connection with a settlement of a group of Angles in the area.

On the medal in figure 17 we find a helmeted warrior. A god does not normally need a helmet, so this medal must have been produced in another society than one in figure 15, probably England. The helmet is a symbol of protection, meaning that the depicted god is offering protection. Since we know that the Wulfings were also called Helmings it is possible that the helmeted god was a Helming. Therefore, the Helming king who distributed the bracteate was probably believed to be of the same descent as the god. Could the king be one of the Helming kings of the Royal House of East Anglia? As Sam Newton has pointed out, Hrotmund could have moved to England with men and gold a few years after AD 515 when Beowulf met him. He could have established a small kingdom in Suffolk, and he would have had first-hand knowledge of the bracteate tradition from the Danish court.

We should not expect the lineage of East Anglia referred to in this chapter to be a strict one. Occasionally, names were deliberately inserted into a lineage to justify the name of the clan. Wuffa means "little wulf" and was probably only introduced because the East Anglian kings were called Wulfings. If two succeeding kings were brothers, there would be room for three kings before Wehha died.
However, it is possible that a second Helming king made this bracteate. Note that the names of the Danish kings begin with the letter H. Alliteration was revered as magic and a H-name implied being "high-born", attesting that the person belonged to the nobility, the warrior class. Hryp was probably the last king in East Anglia who was born in Scandinavia.

On the bracteate (figure 17) we see the twin boys, Romulus and Remus, suckling a she-wolf. The same motif is found on many Roman coins from the time of Emperor Constantine the Great AD 303-337. On the other side of these coins is an image of what could be an adult Romulus or of the Emperor himself. The coins in gold or in bronze were given to Roman soldiers. The Divine Twins were very popular among Roman warriors and Germanic warriors engaged in military service for the Roman emperor, despite the Germanics having their own names for the twins. Nevertheless, the she-wolf on the gold medal signifies that some Angles had adopted the Roman myth of a she-wolf suckling the Divine Twins. The ethnic Wulfings probably believed in this myth, too. Wulfing warriors believed that the Divine Twins could help them in battle, and may even have perceived themselves as incarnations of the Divine Twins.

The eight pointed star beside the god (figure 17) symbolises heaven. That means that he is a spiritual invisible power. The most likely name of this god was Ing, the vigorous Divine Twin worshipped by all Angles. His spirit was supposed to reside in the king. Notice the place name Ingham ("Ing's home") is found in only three places in Britain: one in Suffolk near the site where the gold medal (figure 17) was found. This area is near the River Little Ouse, bordering Suffolk and Norfolk. The Angles who settled here probably came by this very river; the second Ingham is in Norfolk, north of Norwich; and the third one, in north Mercia. In Yorkshire, we find an Ing's Meadow and an Ing's Field, while in Mercia (Nottinghamshire) there is an Ing

18. The reconstructed Anglian village at West Stow around AD 500

Close and an Ing's Holm.

In West Stow, only 2 km from Ingham in northwest Suffolk, an Anglian village from around AD 500 has been excavated and reconstructed (figure 18).

We know of 55 bracteates in England from the period AD 500-575. 29 of them, from Kent, are type D and believed to have been brought by Jutish settlers. The remaining English bracteates have the same motives and belong to the same religious tradition as the Scandinavian, but the style is different from their Scandinavian counterparts. Additionally, the material is mostly silver, suggesting they were mostly produced in England.

Sam Newton has pointed out that several of the royal treasures in the Sutton Hoo ship burial have wolf symbols. The purse in figure 28 shows two wolves often thought to be attacking a man from both sides – they are rather whispering in his ears, guiding him. Some people may think that they look like dogs, but the fore parts of their bodies are so strongly built that they resemble wolves more.

Indeed, the motive of the she-wolf and twins is a recurring one in East Anglia, even found on coins such as those from King Æthelberth of East Anglia from the AD 700s (Newton 1993).

Barwith Syssel

Heathobards are called *Hadbarder* in the Danish legends, taking their name from *had* meaning "fight" and *bard* meaning "axe", hence the name "battleaxe". They were the tribe in Barwith Syssel (figure 7) and, likewise, the name of the syssel comes from *bard* and *with* meaning "woods".

Other people were named after their weapons. Longobard is "long axe". Saxon is "sword man". German is "spear man". The Heathobards had a sacred moor in Ejsbøl, southern Jutland, (figure 7), where opulent war loot was sacrificed around AD 300.

The Heathobards were wealthy legendary warriors. In Saxo Grammaticus' *Deeds of the Danes*, we find the deeds of the Heathobard kings. The king Ingeld was named after Ing. One legend tells of a "common" goldsmith in Ingeld's court who dared to court the queen and, therefore, had some of his hind chopped of. The Heathobards had similar beliefs to the other Angles such as the Divine Twins, as illustrated in the wonderful buckle below (figure 19) from Galsted (figure 7). Unfortunately, the lower part of the buckle is missing.

The Heathobards were the last tribe to offer any resistance to the Danish military pressure on the tribes in Jutland. *Widsith* provides us with some insight again:

Hrothulf and Hrothgar, nephew and uncle,

kept peace together for a very long while,

after they had driven off the tribe of the Wicingas

and humiliated the vanguard of Ingeld

and cut down the host of Heathobardan at Heorot.

The name Hrothgar (in Danish *Roar*) comes from *hroth* meaning "victorious" and *gar* meaning "defender". The Danish king Hrothgar

Fig 19. Buckle from Galsted in Barwith Syssel, AD 400s

probably had his main residence on Funen where the young warrior Beowulf arrived around AD 515. Another Danish king Hrothulf (in Danish *Rolf*) meaning "victorious wolf" was visiting king Hrothgar when Beowulf stayed there. We know from the Roman history writer Jordanes that king Rodulf (Hrothulf) and his men were fighting for King Theodoric the Great, king in Italy AD 493-526, around AD 507. When Hrothulf returned to the Baltic area around AD 510 with a small group of professional warriors he became a powerful king. *Widsith* mentions that he aided his uncle Hrothgar for a while.

At that time, the feud between the Heathobards and the Danes was already ongoing and longstanding, as referenced in Norse Saga literature.

But it is *Beowulf* that is of interest here (lines 57-85):

Haughty Healfdene, who held through life,   57
Sage and sturdy, the Scyldings glad.
Then, one after one, there woke to him,
To the chieftain of clansmen, children four:
Heorogar, then Hrothgar, then Halga brave;
And I heard that -- was -- 's queen,   62
The Heathoscylfing's helpmate dear.
To Hrothgar was given such glory of war,
Such honour of combat, that all his kin
Obeyed him gladly till great grew his band
Of youthful comrades. It came in his mind
To bid his henchmen a hall uprear,
Ia master mead-house, mightier far
Than ever was seen by the sons of earth   70
And within it, then, to old and young
He would all allot that the Lord had sent him,
Save only the land and the lives of his men.
Wide, I heard, was the work commanded,
For many a tribe this mid-earth round,   75
To fashion the folkstead. It fell, as he ordered,
In rapid achievement that ready it stood there,
Of halls the noblest: Heorot he named it
Whose message had might in many a land.
Not reckless of promise, the rings he dealt,   80
Treasure at banquet: there towered the hall,
High, gabled wide, the hot surge waiting
Of furious flame. Nor far was that day
When father and son-in-law stood in feud
For warfare and hatred that woke again.   85

Something is missing in the original line 62:

hyrde ic þæt wæs..... Onelan cwen,

I would argue that Ongenthow's son, Onela, was married to Hrothgar's sister. Onela was the same age as Hrothgar, but the name of his bride is unknown due to the missing information. Onela was a Scylfing like his father Ongentheow as per line 63 (figure 11). Heatho-scylfings were fighting-Scylfings.

The Danish king Healfdene was slain by the Heathobard king Froda in around AD 495. Around five years later, Healfdene's three sons retaliated, invading the Heathobard territory and slewing Froda. Most battles at that time were carried out as surprise attacks at night, most unusally arson attacks on halls. Both Heorogar and Halga fell during this incident, resulting in Hrothgar becoming the leading Danish king. Hrothgar is praised in lines 64-66. Halga (*heil-ger* = "useful spear") did not belong to the Scyldings. When his father, the Wulfing king Helm, was killed, Halga was fostered by the Danish king Healfdene and became a famous Danish warrior king.

In lines 67-82, we hear that Hrothgar planned and had built a marvellous mead-house that he called Heorot. Heorot means *hart*, the male stag, and it is possible that the hall was placed where the village of Harte now lies in Barwith Syssel (figure 7). Many tribes took part in the building of the hall. Line 82 describes how the hall was adorned with antlers. In Jutland, the young stag was a symbol of the heavenly father also called *Bull* or *Tiw*. Hrothgar probably choose the name Heorot because he intended to get support from the tribes in Jutland. West of Harte is Trældiget, a 15 km long bank with a moat dating from ca. AD 500. It was a defence against enemies from the west, probably the Heathobards. Incidentally, "mid-earth", mentioned in line 75, is the human world between heaven and underworld.

The plans for Heorot ran into trouble because a monster named

Grendel, who lived in the moor-land for twelve years, attacked Heorot at night, killing Hrothgar's men. The name Grendel is related to *grind* and probably means "giant". "Grind" is a male name in both Old English and Swedish. The myth might be a reference to guerrilla warfare from inhabitants around Heorot. They attacked at night and King Hrothgar could not sleep there. The hall was built on Heathobardan territory. Beowulf was called to Heorot in order to slay Grendel, and Grendel actually received a fatal wound, but his mother, a witch, came to Heorot at night and kidnapped some Thanes (perhaps renegades?). Beowulf had to go out on the moor, where she lived and slay her. Here he also found Grendel's body and brought the head of the body home to Heorot. Grendel's mother is quite likely the traditional Mother Earth. She was worshipped in Jutland by sacrifices on the moors but the tradition died out in the 5th century AD when many Angles migrated. *Beowulf's* description of the brilliant life at Heorot, compared to the life of the outcasts in the moor-land, gives an idea of why the traditional tribal sacrifices on moors disappeared.

When Beowulf visited Heorot he heard that Hrothgar's daughter, Freawaru, would be given in marriage to Ingeld, son of the Heathobard king Froda, as a peace offering between the Danes and the Heathobards. *Beowulf* lines 2024 and following are:

Hrothgar's daughter Freawaru
To nobles continuously bore the ale-flagon,
She is promised, young, gold-adorned,
To gracious <u>son of Froda. This has arranged</u>
<u>The Friend of the Scyldings the kingdom's shepherd,</u>
<u>And counsel reckons it, that he with this woman</u>
<u>A great part of the slaughter-feuds conflicts would settle.</u>

He foretells, however, that an old warrior will encourage a young

Heathobard king to avenge his father's death against the son of the Danish man who killed his father and who struts about in his Heathobardish war-gear; lines 82-85 foretell that Heorot will be burned in a war between a father and a son-in-law. The allusion to the burning of Heorot refers to the Heathobard campaign against Heorot under the leadership of Ingeld; Heorot does indeed burn and is destroyed, but the Danes are victorious over the Heathobards.

From both the *Widsith* and *Beowulf* poems, we learn that the Danish king Hrothgar defeated the Heathobardan king Ingeld ca. AD 520. Ingeld, called Withergeld, "the avenger", by the Danes, was not killed. Ingeld and his housecarls probably attacked Heorot, burning it before organising the emigration of the Heathobards. As the Heathobards are called Wikings in *Widsith*, they were probably familiar with long sea journeys.

When the Heathobards embarked on their migration around AD 520 most of England was already inhabited by other Angles. They had to settle at the very north. Here, they established a kingdom named Bernicia, a name related to the bards. Berwick in Bernicia was previously called Bardowic. Howick, also in Bernicia, is reminiscent of Ho Bay on the west cost of Barwith Syssel. In Bernicia, we find the place name Ingram, and in the Bernician royal genealogies, names such as Ingibrand, Inguec and Ingui – all related to the popular Anglian god Ing – occur. Ida, king of Bernicia from AD 547, had a great-grandfather named Ingui. If the source is reliable, Ingui would have been king in AD 490 and not the same person as Ingeld. Ing-ui or Ing-wi means "Ing dedicated" and Ing-eld means "Ing mighty". It is possible that Ingui is Froda because the god Ing was went by the name Frey, and Froda is called after Frey.

Legends about Ingeld were preserved in Northumberland. In AD 797, a priest, Alcuin, wrote a letter to the monks in Lindisfarne in which he blamed them for listening to the heathen poem *Hieneldus*.

He said: *Quid eium Hinieldus cum Cristo (What has Ingeld to do with Christ?).* Unfortunately, the poem is now lost, but the Danish monk, Saxo, read it sometime around AD 1200 and recorded it in Latin. Danish folklorist Axel Olrik (d. 1917) later translated it into English. Strophes 18 and 19, respectively, read:

A cruel fate has befallen Fróthi's kinsmen
when the king was given such a coward as heir:
no greater worth hast thou than a hunted goat,
or than sheep in shambles shrinking in terror.

Shall Sverting's seed hold sway over Denmark,
Seated at Leire with Saxon warriors,
on thy lap whilst thou fondlest the linen-clad woman,
the fair-haired daughter of thy father's banesman

The entire poem is the speech of an old warrior about the ideals of a warrior society. He blames Ingeld for luxurious living, cowardliness and for not seeking vengeance for the killing of his father, Frothi. Hrothgar is called Sverting ("incendiary"). In a Scandinavian epos, Freawaru is called Hrut (or Heorot), named after her father's mead-house. At the end of the poem, Ingeld stands up with his sword and disowns his bride, which means war.

At Yeavering (Northumberland), a seventh-century royal estate of the kings of Bernicia has been identified from place name evidence and the testimony of the Venerable Bede. The 'township' was made up in each phase of a major timber-built hall, a few smaller buildings including a temple (later church), a timber grandstand and a large enclosure next to the residential complex. The successive timber halls of the early and mid-600s are the largest domestic structures uncovered to date on any early Anglo-Saxon site. With their internal length of c. 25 m and their floor areas of 260 and 290 m2, respectively, each could have accommodated up to 60 men.

Fenced enclosures were attached to the main hall in each phase, and like the partitions inside the halls, they hint at social and functional differentiations among the residents. The grandstand's capacity of approx. 150 people indicates the size of the group or groups assembled here, probably for council meetings, highlighting the function of this estate as an administrative centre (Hope-Taylor 1977).

Origin of the Angles

Our interest here is finding the origin of the Angles and identifying the origin of their ideas. It is a difficult task as they committed nothing to writing. We only have archaeological finds on which to base our investigations. The tribes in southern Jutland (figure 7) seem to have had similar ideas and adored the same god, Ing. After they migrated to England, they were all called Angles. It is possible that a tribe in Anglen was also called Angles. The traditions of the Angles can be traced back to what archaeologists call the Großromstedt Culture named after a cemetery with 600 graves in Großromstedt, Thüringia. These graves are the result of a massacre of some Germanic tribes by the Roman army 11 BC. Thirty of the graves displayed a pair of drinking horn mountings which lends considerable weight to the belief that these Germanic tribes worshipped the Divine Twins. Other finds from the Großromstedt graves are typical of Germanic finds in Thüringia and areas along the Elbe River.

A very impressive cult site belonging to the Großromstedt Culture was found in a moor, in Oberdorla, Thüringia. Here, 70 cult sites were separated with fences. Many of them had rude wooden idols, mostly female, and some shaped phalli. Figure 20 shows the most delicate idol (Behm-Blancke 2002). Large amounts of animal and human remains indicate that sacrifices were made. The site was in use ca. 500 BC to AD 600. Cult sites in moors such as those in southern Jutland and Thüringia indicate a similar method of worshipping a goddess.

The Elbe-Germanic tribes including the Angles called themselves Svebic (``kinsmen''). In AD 9, three Roman legions were wiped out in a battle with a Svebic army at Teutoburger Wald. After that incident, the Romans sought revenge against the Germanic tribes settled between the Rhine and the Elbe (see the chapter entitled *The Origin of the Long Horn*). In the end, the Romans gave up trying to conquer the land and instead tried to bribe Svebic chieftains, but the Svebes forbade all import of Roman luxuries. In fact, there are remarkably few Roman luxuries in the Elbe-Germanic graves. Indeed, no rich prince graves have been found at all in southern Jutland. In these times of constant threat of war, the Svebic tribes would have needed some sort of military organisation. However, it seems that some of the Svebic tribes were *not* organised by a powerful prince; rather, they were organised according to ethnic relations and common religious rituals.

In some of his letters, the Roman Lucius Seneca (4 BC-AD 65) describes the fate of Germanic tribes. He reports that in his time there were large displacements of Germanic tribes. When a tribe was defeated they had three possibilities: they could migrate to another area, where they were allowed to settle; they could assimilate themselves into the victorious tribe; or they could be wiped out. In fact, the Roman Tacitus refers how the Brukter tribe was wiped out by other Germanic tribes.

Some of the Elbe-Germanic people, who

Fig 20.
Open-air idol from Oberdorla, Thür-
ingia, height 32
cm, AD 200s

called themselves Angles, seem to have migrated north. On Ptolemy's map from AD 130, the Angles are placed on the left bank of the Elbe River, south of modern-day Hamburg. Tacitus puts them in roughly the same place in AD 100. At that time, there is an increase in the population in Istathe Syssel due to the invading Angles. This could not have happened without fighting. Moreover, scorched villages are found in Istathe Syssel dating from the turn of the first millennium. The new buildings were of a new style, which resembled the old home of the Angles by the Elbe River. The Olgerdike in Jutland, build in AD 31 by the Angles against invading settlers and thieves from the north, was renewed 100 years later (figure 7).

In AD 150, the sacrifices in the Torsbjerg Moor changed from being agricultural products to weapons. Torsbjerg Moor is situated in that part of Istathe Syssel still called Anglen and this moor must have been a sacred site for the Angles. The Angles held ostentatious religious rituals in the nearby village of Brarup. In the AD 400s, when many Angles migrated, the sacrifices in Torsbjerg Moor come to an end.

The Heathobards were part of Anglian culture but they might also have been part of the Longobards, who, according to Ptolemy, resided by the Elbe River. In that case, the invasion in Barwith Syssel was probably before the invasion of Istathe Syssel. We do not know what happened to the original tribal population in southern Jutland. The continued use of sacred sites such as Torsbjerg Moor suggests some kind of assimilation must have occurred. On the other hand, the fortified walls imply warfare. Perhaps the local tribes in southern Jutland were already opponents? Anglian military techniques were more advanced; consequently, whenever they settled near a local tribe, they offered some level of "protection" to the local tribe against their neighbours.

Fig 21. Pots used for grave gifts.
a) Oberdorla, Thüringia, ca. AD 200 (Behm-Blancke 2002).
b) Hjemsted, southern Jutland, ca. AD 450 (Ethelberg 1986)

Around AD 200, some tribes here called the Angles had established themselves in southern Jutland as is marked by distinctive pottery in that area. Their culture also seems to have influenced neighbouring areas such as Funen and Holstein. An example of the pottery is seen in figure 21 b. This pot is typical of the cemeteries in Hjemsted, Ellem Syssel (figure 7). The inhumations were orientated east-west, the body placed on its side facing south, with grave gifts like the pot here arranged in front of the body.

From around AD 275, war booty is deposited in Ejsbøl Moor, near Haderslev. The Angles lost a great sea battle to a tribe from the north. There is reference to a legend, which provides a possible description of this battle, in the chapter on the East Saxons. According to the legend, Balder was king of the Angles at that time, and after the defeat the Angles had much less influence.

The two pots shown in figure 21 have the same decoration: three lines in a zigzag pattern. This is an indication that the Angles in

Slesvig-Holstein brought some of their culture and beliefs with them from Thüringia. This type of decoration on funerary pots is very old and common for several Germanic people. The three line symbol has a religious meaning, perhaps representing the three forces in life. The gold horns offer a careful explanation of the idea of the three forces of life, which will be examined in later chapters, but for now it is important to note that the three goddesses of fate are representations of the three forces of life.

There were many migrations along the Elbe River. At the beginning of the first millennium, the Angles emigrated from Thüringia, down the Saale River and the Elbe to Slesvig-Holstein. This emigration can be traced, for instance, in place names ending in *-leben* in Thüringia, *-lev* in Jutland and later *-low* in England. It is likely that they brought knowledge of alphabets with them. It is commonly accepted that the runic alphabet of 24 runes was invented in Slesvig -Holstein around AD 150, almost certainly inspired by north alpine alphabets. The basic idea of the runic alphabet is the three forces of life, which will be explored in a later chapter.

The Anglian tribes fought with tribes to the north and south, as evident in their sacrifices of weapon in moors. In AD 400, when the time of great migrations began in earnest, fighting increased. Several old poems and sagas have legends of heroic kings from this period. One such king was Offa, described as a Danish hero by Saxo. Saxo refers to a legend of Offa and another king named Hading (probably a Heathobard from Barwith Syssel). According to the legend, they ravaged and plundered each other's land. Another threat came from the Danish kings of eastern Denmark, who drove away the chieftains (*Erils*) from Jutland and established kings of their own lineage. Moreover, the climate grew colder at this time, causing a decrease in agricultural production and making cattle and slave raids more enticing than fighting. Taken together, these

Angles in England

For the purpose of simplification, that part of England south of the Thames is called Saxon and the rest, Anglian, here. Both areas differed in culture at the Time of the Great Migrations, AD 375-575. The use of clasps on the sleeves of women's clothing is particular to the English Angles, demonstrating that they brought some of their culture from Scandinavia with them. The clasp fashion was inspired by southwestern Norway and Denmark and spread from Norfolk all over Anglian England. Saxon women did not use clasps as their dresses were more peplos-like, fastened at the shoulders with two brooches. The Angles typically used a cruciform brooch to fasten their capes.

Germanic immigrants in England brought their own architecture, pottery, jewellery, language, runes and religion with them. In many

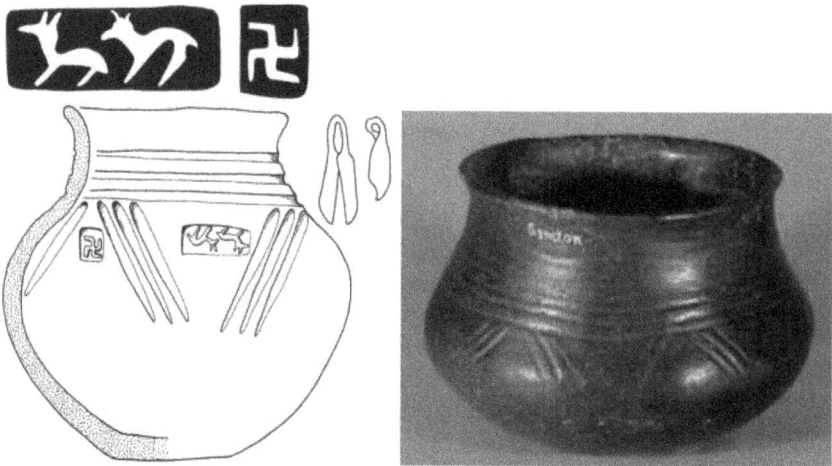

Fig 22. Urn from Spong Hill, North Elmham, Norfolk (Myres and Green 1973) and urn from Sancton, Yorkshire (Myres and Southern 1973), AD 400s

cases, the shape of the pottery was the same as that of the Angles in southern Jutland and the English Angles. The same can be said about the decoration on the pottery. For instance, the decorating of funeral pottery with three lines was a tradition, which the Angles clearly brought to England. Compare the decorations on the pots figure 21 and figure 22: the three line symbol gives us an idea of the beliefs of the English Angles.

It has been pointed out (Myres 1986) that one of the urns from Caistor-by-Norwich, Norfolk, came from the same workshop as that, which made two other urns for cemeteries in Holstein and Slesvig. The cremation urns from the Anglian cemetery at Sancton, Yorkshire, have too many close parallels with the corresponding pottery from Borgstedt in Istathe Syssel (figure 7) to be purely coincidental.

Some of the Elbe-Germanics that lived by the lower Elbe around AD 400 may have referred to themselves as Angles. We know that they migrated into East Anglia at least. A cemetery at Issendorf, to the left of the lower Elbe, contained 5500 urn graves from the period AD 380-550. Some of the urns are so similar to urns found at the cemetery at Spong Hill in East Anglia that they must have been made by the same potter. Furthermore, the style of the jewellery in the graves at Issendorf bears close relation to the Elbe-Germanics in Thüringia.

Exploring the religious ideas of the pre-Christian Anglo-Saxon culture is difficult as the heathen Anglo-Saxons did not use writing, and the surviving runic inscriptions are very few and brief. Most of the inscriptions have been lost because the runes were inscribed on wood or leather. But, thankfully, pottery and grave finds of metal objects were decorated with picture symbols, which obviously had a religious meaning.

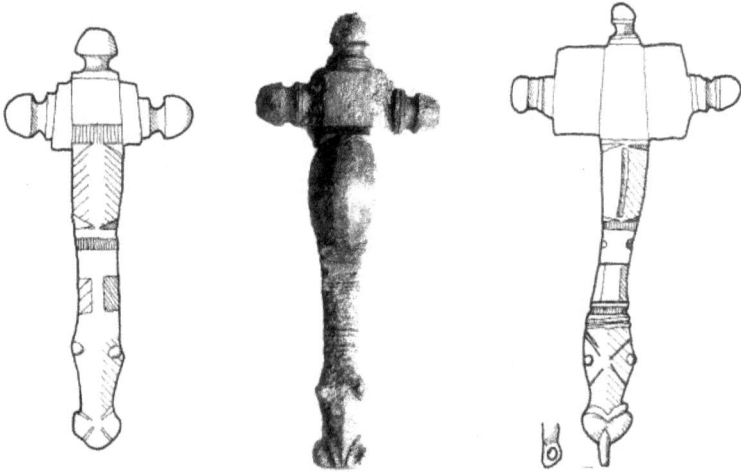

Fig 23. Cruciform brooches, around AD 500: a) Olde, Norway;
b) Dankirke, southern Jutland; c) Wakerley, North Hampshire (Hines 1984)

Cruciform brooches evolved in Holstein and Scandinavia in the course of the AD 400s. The first cruciform brooches, brought to and made in England by Anglian and Jutish settlers, were closely similar to their continental counterparts. In England, they are found predominantly in East Anglia, but also in Kent, the east Midlands and as far north as the Humber. This brooch was made mostly in the period AD 475-525. The three cruciform brooches in figure 23 were not imported. They were produced by local craftsmen. Remarkably, five cruciform brooches like those in figure 23 b were found in a pile in Dankirke, in Ellem Syssel, (figure 7). Typically, only a single brooch is found in female graves. Dankirke was a rich village in the period AD 300-500 with trade and craftsmen. Only part of the village has been excavated, but 38 Roman coins have been found to date as well as many remains of iron production near the village.

The cruciform brooches obviously have a common symbolism. Generally, the heathen cross is a symbol of the spiritual world. However, the large monster is a symbol of the forces in the realm of death. The three knobs on the head-plate probably represent the forces in the world of the living. Like the three line symbol, they symbolise the three forces in life. The square head-plate probably denotes life itself. Life was understood as a circle similar to the circulation of the sun, night and day. The deceased might be reborn, usually into their own tribe.

The serpent-like monster of the foot-plate probably represents the earth with its destructive and generative forces. The earth is the foundation of life. The serpent of the underworld is pictured on the gold horn. The pearl in its mouth is a symbol of the soul about to be reborn. In Jutland, funeral pottery with serpents have been found (see also the carved stone in figure 54). The serpent symbol will be described in a later chapter.

The brooches seem to be markers of group identity and common religious belief as does the burial places of the Angles. Indeed, the substantial number of immigrants in the AD 400s came in ethnic groups that originated in small areas on the Continent. Each ethnic group settled in a small area in England. For instance, the people from Ellem Syssel settled in part of Norfolk. The 2259 cremation burials at Spong Hill correspond to a local population of 400 persons. 227 of the cremations included bones of a cremated horse. These graves belonged to small landowners, not the elite. About 15% of the graves contained weapons. There is no indications of a warrior elite or fighting between the small landowners in the AD 400s. The British population of East Anglia was thin and the Angles did not have to fight them. Certainly, it was particularly appropriate for such a society of new settlers to maintain the traditional culture from the old land.

During the Roman era, the Germanics lived in tribal societies, with the ethnic groups living together in local communities. The members of the groups helped and protected each other. Important decisions were made at gatherings of representatives. According to Tacitus, fields belonged to the community and domestic animals belonged to families. Even if some young men participated in warfare abroad, they did not become a warrior class. Some tribes had a chieftain called an "eril" or "gode". Other tribes, including some Danish groups, had a king. We will see that the long golden horn belonged to one such traditional culture. The settlements in England resemble the settlements in the old land (figures 10 and 18), suggesting that much of the culture of the old land was also maintained in England in the AD 400s.

Social stratification

Around AD 500, a second migration occurred. The 57 inhumation burials at Spong Hill occurred around AD 500-575. They correspond to roughly 30 living persons or approximately 5 families. These graves are richer, implying that the wealthy group probably arrived from abroad and acquired elite status. The Benedictine Monk Matthew of Paris records in his *Chronica Majora* that in the year AD 527, many Germanic petty chiefs arrived in East Anglia and Mercia.

The emergence of inhumation burials in the Anglian cemeteries is a sign of social stratification. Contrary to cremation, inhumation facilitates the possibility of contact to the soul of the deceased and even ancestor worship. Inhumations can include valuable belongings of the deceased, and the grave may represent the status of the family. Inhumation seems to become more widespread as the family unit becomes more important than the community.

In Tyttel's Halh, 9 km west of Spong Hill, is a cemetery founded in the late AD 400s, which contained 28 inhumation burials. One boy's grave included part of a sword scabbard and in the well-furnished women's graves were British types of textiles and British types of beads (Walton Rogers 2013), implying that the men of the households were armed Germanic settlers from abroad, while the women were wealthy British natives.

The newcomers had a different culture and settled near an ethnic community that they did not belong to. Furthermore, people moved around and the community was a mix of foreigners, some of British background. Given this situation, it was difficult for the ethnic group to make decisions for the local population. Instead of ethnic gatherings, gatherings of local inhabitants may have been held. The strongest and richest families in the area would have controlled such a development; the weakening of the ethnic community led to social stratification.

Part of the native British population disappeared from the areas where Angles and Saxons lived. The two peoples in East and West England were separated by vast forests. Their language and religion were different. Archaeological finds confirms that there was no trade between the two peoples.

Examination of Y-chromosomes of the contemporary English population and the north Welsh population have shown that they have very little conformity, indicating that there was never close contact between the two populations (Weale 2002). On the whole, the British absolutely hated the Anglo-Saxons and refused to have much contact with them.

The British monk Gildas wrote an account of the arrival of the Anglo-Saxons to Britain in *The Conquest and Ruin of Britain*. He describes "the ferocious Saxons, hated by man and God", who came as mercenaries and "devastated town and country". Gildas describes a British victory over the Anglo-Saxons around AD 510, but at the time of writing – the AD mid-500s – "the cities of our land are deserted, in ruins and unkempt".

The "Wasteland" may have another reason. In AD 540, there was a worldwide climate catastrophe (Keys 2000), probably caused by the huge eruption of the volcano Llopango in El Salvador. This resulted in crop failure and famine as the sun darkened for a year and a half due to dust in the atmosphere. The Roman historian and statesman Cassiodorus referred to a dimming of the sun: "we have had a spring without mildness and a summer without heat ... The months which should have been maturing the crops have been chilled by north winds. Rain is denied and the reaper fears new frosts". Tree-ring evidence from the British Isles shows that tree growth was slow in the period AD 535-555.

The famine also led to the spread of the bubonic plague starting in the Middle East. The plague reached the shores of the British Isles in AD 547, but it affected only the British people, who had good connections to the Mediterranean Area. Furthermore, the British population was denser in villages, where the chance of infection was greater. It is probable that more than 60% of the population died. In legends from this time, the Celtic British area is described as a "Wasteland". Even the famous British warrior King Arthur died from the plague. The Anglo-Saxons eventually invaded the area. And in AD 650, only Wales and Cornwall were outside of Anglo-Saxon control. These events also contributed to the death of the Celtic languages in England.

Essentially:
In AD 535 & 536, extreme weather likely led to a great famine and thereby a population loss.
In AD 547, Anglo-Saxons established Bernicia, appropriating part of a Celtic area called Bryneich.
Around AD 549, a great plague caused much population loss.
Around AD 560, Anglians, led by Aella, conquered all of east Yorkshire and the British kingdom of Ebrauc, establishing Deira in its place.
In AD 573, was the Battle of Arfderydd at Arthuret in Cumbria, Welsh fought Welsh, which weakened the Celtic Welsh.
In AD 581, Aella of Deira seized land from the Britons, thereby establishing or enlarging Deira. He conquered a realm of the Britons and the town of York.
Finally, around AD 584, the kingdom of the Iclingas became Mercia.
The battles between Angles and Britons in Deira may be the background for an account from Rome around AD 590 in which Pope

Gregory the Great met some slave boys with blonde hair. They told him they were Angles and their king was Aelle, but the Pope believed them to be Angels, causing him to send the missionaries to Britain in AD 595. The Pope intended to make York the second archbishopric after Canterbury and bishop Paulinus was sent by the Pope, under the title of Bishop of York, but he stayed in Kent because the Christian influence in Northumberland was weak. He was later canonised.

The royal seat of Deira was situated by the River Derwent, east of York, as was the king's pagan temple at Goodmanham. This is consistent with the archaeological record which shows the greatest concentration of early Anglian cemeteries in the east, such as those at Sancton and Londesborough and the early Anglian barrow burials at Driffield and Uncleby. In AD 627, Paulinus came to Deira with Edwin, the king of Deira due to military help from Redwald, the powerful king of East Anglia. Edwin was then baptised by Paulinus and Paulinus pronounced Bishop of York by Edwin. They burned down the pagan temple, which was surrounded with high hoarding, and began building a church.

The strides between the tiny Germanic chiefdoms and against the Britons led to the forming of slightly larger units and by AD 520 there were small kingdoms. The famine led to plundering, war and the emergence of new rulers in many places around the world. In Anglo-Saxon England, reduced resources and increased insecurity reinforced the forming of larger kingdoms such as East Anglia and Mercia. Wehha was the first king of East Anglia after the union of Norfolk and Suffolk, which may have occurred in AD 560. He died AD 571.

Despite the climatic catastrophe of AD 540 being significant for the birth of England, there were other circumstances, too. When conquering the Wasteland in Britain, the Anglo Saxons used the opportunity to settle in new land, using military power to drive out the inhabitants. The Germanics may have had an urge for freedom that led to migrations. This urge was predominantly felt by the younger generations who did not have the right of succession in the traditional Germanic family. They left home and joined the army or settled abroad.

Returning to the Angles, square-headed brooches were the most expensive and complex items of jewellery used by Germanics during the migration period. More than 200 were found in England (Hines 1997). They were all produced by local craftsmen. These brooches, such as the one above, with square-head and two creatures licking the diamond-food originated in southern Scandinavia in the first half of the AD 400s. Many square-headed brooches have been found in

Fig 24. Square-headed brooch from Fairford, Luton. Guilt bronze. Drilled holes suggest repair in antiquity (Hines 1997)

Denmark and southern Norway.

Around AD 500, the fashion for square-headed brooches came to Kent and the Anglian zone, probably via a secondary wave of higher-status immigrants from southern Scandinavia. At this time, more families from the chieftain class of southern Jutland were partaking in the migration. It is likely that they re-established their form of social system in England as well as their status symbol: the square-headed brooch.

These brooches were worn by women of families of very high social status. They were used in the period AD 500-570 when power was more and more unevenly distributed. The numbers of these brooches declined in AD 550-570, probably due to the social elite becoming more restricted and closed. The graves after AD 550 are less richly furnished than those of the earlier period. The later square-headed brooches may have been used by remnants of an old high-status group losing power or transforming itself into a new elite with new habits. Note that around AD 560, the kingdoms of Deira and East Anglia were established and soon after Mercia emerged.

Square-headed brooches were used the same way as their more modest predecessors, the cruciform brooches; generally just one fastened on a heavy outer cloak at chest height. In the graves, they are placed almost horizontally like in figure 24. Such positioning can be seen in several contemporary depictions of women. In figure 50, we see two of the thousands of gold foil figures called *guldgubber* in Danish, which have been found. They were used for worshipping a goddess and depict the goddess and/or the adorer. Here, we see the goddess wearing a large square-headed brooch.

Despite the square-headed brooches all having different details, they all have the similar symbolism and, in general, resemble the idea of the cruciform brooches. On the square-headed brooch in figure 24 we can see the serpent monster on the foot-plate, but the three forces of life are introduced as the two eyes and nose of the monster. On the Fairford brooch, the three forces are pictured as heads – probably representing the three goddesses of fate. The heads of the monsters on the square-headed brooches always have two smaller biting monsters on the back. They are guiding the larger monster and represent the Divine Twins. A similar symbol on the gold horn will further explain this later.

The inside of the large monster represents the lower world, under the surface of the earth. Here lies the site of regeneration. Some brooches have human bodies or faces in this area. In figure 24, we have a head inside the monster probably representing deceased souls passing through the realm of the dead on their way to being reborn.

The head-plate symbolises the upper world, or rather the invisible spiritual part of it. In the middle, we have two eyes of the generating goddess. This goddess of life gives birth to all creatures. The Angles called her *Eostra* or *Easter*. She appears as the morning light of the eastern sky. She was worshipped at sunrise and at a springtime festival. She is often symbolised by two eyes rising from the earth. The eyes perhaps signifying shining celestial bodies.

If we look again at the head-plate in figure 24, we see that the part with the eyes in the middle is surrounded by two outer spheres of spiritual life. In the outermost sphere, we find some powerful protective spirits, possibly ancestors or legendary heroes. In the corners, we find two masks with bird-beaks, perhaps representing the Divine Twins.

The advanced square-headed brooches are very focused on the

spiritual world and the ancestors. It is typical for the elite in societies with inequalities to use some ideology or their heritage for legitimatising their power.

The square-headed brooches still adored the goddesses of faith of the lower world, although this idea seems to become obsolete among the elite around AD 570, when the square-headed brooches went out of fashion.

Thanks to the Northumbrian monk, the Venerable Bede, we are fortunate to have the name of the great goddess of the Angles. In 710, Bede wrote a treatise entitled *The Reckoning of Time*, where he describes the heathen Anglo-Saxon names of the months:

Eosturmonath [April] has a name which is now translated as "Paschal month",
and which was once called after a goddess of theirs named *Eostre*, in whose
honour feasts were celebrated in that month. Now they designate that Paschal
season by her name, calling the joys of the new rite by the time-honoured
name of the old observance.

Paschal is an archaic English form of the Hebrew word *pesah*. Bede further explains that the Insular church inculturated the name "Easter" from a heathen festival for the prime Christian springtime festival.

In England, a few locations bear witness to the worship of Eostra: Eastry in Kent, Eastra in Cambridgeshire and Austerfield in Yorkshire. It is peculiar that 16 place names in East Anglia begin with *east* and only 5 begin with *west*. Could it be that some of the original *east* names were related to the Anglian goddess Eostra?

When the Anglo-Saxons were Christianised in the AD 600s, their faith in the goddess Eostre gradually disappeared, but she was still worshipped in southern Jutland until Denmark was Christianised around AD 1000. Delineations of the goddess can be seen on some sceattas minted in Ribe around AD 710 (figure 7). Sceattas are small silver coins minted at Germanic trading centres around the North Sea. In the AD 600s and 700s, Frisians, Anglo-Saxons and Jutes developed a common culture. They shared the same language, techniques and social system. The Frisians were the first to make cloth of wool for sails and build sailing ships. They traded cloth, slaves and Frankish swords. Some of the first sceattas were minted in the AD 680s in the Frisian town of Dorestad just south of Utrecht. Other early mint centres were Ipswich in East Anglia and Domburg on the Frisian island of Walcheren. In AD 705, a craft and trading centre was established at Ribe, Denmark, inspired by the Dorestad.

In figure 25, we see the front of three sceattas to the left. The two upper ones were found in Jutland and the lower one was found in

Fig 25. Three sceattas of the so called Wodan/Monster type, AD 710

Cambridgeshire, but they were possibly all minted in Ribe. The name Wodan/Monster for this type is a misunderstanding. We see the two eyes of the goddess rise up from the sea. Light rays radiate from the eyes, perhaps representing celestial bodies. The even-armed cross is an old heathen symbol for the spiritual heavenly world. On the outer ring, we see some male faces. They probably have a similar meaning as the faces on the head plate (figure 24) – the spirits of ancestors. The snakes are invisible forces. Another example of this Germanic Goddess can be seen on mountings from the AD 400s (figure 33), which will be explained later.

The Goddess of Light was worshipped in southern Jutland as late as AD 960. This is documented by a report from an Arabic merchant, At -Tartuschi, who visited Hedeby in Istathe Syssel around that year. One of the things he mentions is that the inhabitants worship "al Shira", with the exception of a little group of Christians, who have a church there. He was there when everyone celebrated the goddess by eating and drinking. Those who sacrifice an animal (ox, ram, goat or pig) put the head of the animal on top of a pole outside the front door. The name "al Shira" means "The Shining One" and it is also the Arabic name for the star "Sirius".

The Sutton Hoo ship-burial

The Sutton Hoo grave site contained about twenty barrows and was reserved for people who were buried individually with objects that indicated an exceptional wealth or prestige, probably members of the royal family of East Anglia. It was used in this way from around AD 575 to 625. The ship-burial is one of the most magnificent archaeological finds in England due to its size and completeness and the quality and beauty of its contents. The exceptional artefacts show us elements of the heathen religion of the Anglians before the arrival of Christianity and the Aesir religion.

The Frankish coins, found in the belt purse, testify that the grave belonged to Redwald, king of Anglia AD 615-628. Redwald means "victorious ruler". He also held the title Bretwalda, "Britain's ruler", signifying that he was leader of a dozen kings in the Germanic part of Britain. The ship in which Redwald was buried had room for 38 oars. His body as well as jewellery, weapons and regalia were placed in a wooden hut in the middle of the ship. Ship-burials were heathen, the symbolism being that the spirit of the deceased could sail on the spiritual ship to the realm of the dead. Ship-burials from the AD 600s are only found in East Anglia and in the Vendel area 100 km north of contemporary Stockholm.

The Vendel ship-graves have close archaeological parallels to the Sutton Hoo ship-burial, particularly in the helmet (figure 4). Helmets of a similar shape were used by the cavalry of the Byzantine Army in the AD 500s and the Swedes may have taken part in the wars of this army. They copied the form of the helmets but the decorations are clearly Scandinavian. Mouldings for stamping bronze plates for these helmets have been found on the island of Öland in the Baltic Sea. The helmets found in Vendel may have been produced on Öland.

There are several reports of these helmets from the AD 500s. It is said that a magnificent helmet was given to Beowulf by King Hrothgar. The helmet was called a boar. Beowulf carried this helmet when he fought Grendel's mother. Eadgils (Adils), who became king of Sweden around AD 535 with Beowulf's help, also possessed a boar-helmet called *Hildesvin* ("battle–boar"). According to Snorre, he seized the helmet from another king. According to Saxo, Hrothulf (Rolf Krake) then tried to rob the helmet from Adils. The boar symbol was used by Danish and Swedish kings in the AD 500s. The Sutton Hoo helmet has boar heads on the eyebrows (figure 4), and the helmet from the barrow in Benty Grange, Derbyshire, is boar-crested (figure 66).

We can speculate on how Danes or Swedes brought their helmet tradition to East Anglia. In the latter half of the AD 500s, the East Anglian royal family probably had contact to the rich Swedish kings. The shield from Sutton Hoo was reconstructed and appears to be an older artefact when it was placed in the grave. A similar shield with splendid decorations was found in a Vendel grave in Sweden and suggest personal contact with the Baltic Area. One possibility is that a boy from the East Anglian royal family was fostered by a Swedish king. He could also have been in the military service of a Swedish king in the same manner as Beowulf was with the Danish king. After some years of military service, he may have returned to East Anglia with his men including craftsmen. Perhaps he was married to a Swedish princess? We do not know the name of Redwald's wife, but she was mentioned to be a hard core heathen.

AD 575 marks the end of the Migration Age and about that time there was a fundamental change in Germanic elite culture throughout Europe. The decorative animal style changed from Style 1 into the more sophisticated Style 2. The use of gold bracteates in Scandinavia ceased. The reason for this change is obscure. It may have been a consequence of the climatic catastrophe in AD 540 and the famine that followed. These crises caused some elite groups to lose power. The elite groups that then gained power seem to drop the ethnic connection to their subordinates and instead focused on family and cultivated connections to foreign elite groups. In other words, tribal society was abandoned.

Fig 26. Mythical eagle on the shield of Sutton Hoo. The face on the leg is copied

At the end of the Migration Age, the Frankish rulers and the Swedish rulers turned out to be the most powerful and rich Germanics. These places attracted artisans and splendid examples of style 2 have been found there. The Frankish influence is seen in Kent and the Swedish influence is seen in East Anglia.

A more detailed exploration of the objects from Sutton Hoo offers a greater understanding of the religious ideas of the royal court. The pair of drinking horns have already been mentioned (figure 3) as has the decorated bronze-helmet (figure 4). Both finds are related to the worship of the Divine Twins. The royal sceptre (figure 59) is also important, but the interpretation of the sceptre is covered in the later chapter on Tiw. For now, the focus will be on the mythical eagle on the king's shield.

The characteristic mythical eagle with its rolled up beak and claws can be traced back to the Scythian and Sarmatian tribes where a gold eagle adorned many warrior standards, weapons and jewellery. The eagle symbol was very popular among Sarmatian warriors and was probably the most common animal in the Sarmatian animal style. It symbolised the mistress of heaven who brought the dead soul of the warrior to the realm of death. In Roman times, the Sarmatian warrior elite had considerable influence on some Germanic tribes. Around AD 300, the eagle symbol spread to the warrior elite in some Germanic tribes such as the Goths and Saxons. Since then, eagle symbols have been used on royal coats of arms and is still used today in national symbols for Germany and USA. Around AD 600, the mythical eagle is seen on the Baltic Islands in Scandinavia and even in Sutton Hoo (figure 26 and 27).

The body of the bird (figure 26) is a reconstruction. The bird has female indicators: the decorated costume resembles a woman's dress and cloak. In Norse mythology, the goddess Freya had a mantle of falcon feathers. The eyes and especially the eyebrows are big and they show that she is watching everything. The beak and claws are quite long and have to be rolled up, when not in use. They are long in order to reach out and catch souls. At the back of her head, we have a monster that seems to be interested in consuming souls, possibly a symbol of the large monster in the realm of death that we have seen on the cruciform brooches (figure 23). The crest on the helmet from Sutton Hoo is probably the same monster of death (figure 4).

The mask on the leg of the eagle is very interesting. It is a male face with a beard of glass or precious stones held by silver threads. The same element is seen on most finds of the mythical eagle symbol. The mask probably represents the soul of a deceased human, and the symbol on the shield may testify to the king trusting the mistress of heaven. It may also be that the king had the protection of the goddess of life and death, giving him divine power. On the marvellous belt purse from Sutton Hoo, two of the golden decorations show the mythical eagle bent over another bird with a wide beak – perhaps a mother protecting her young offspring. A bird

Fig 27. Lid from a belt purse, where King Redwald kept his gold

with a wide beak is also seen on the nose and eyebrows of the helmet (figure 4). Such a young bird may represent Eostra, the goddess of dawn. She brings the morning light and new life. Eostra was the goddess of birth for the Angles. The two goddesses are two aspects of the goddess of life.

The Venerable Bede tells us that February was called *Hreth-monath* and March, *Eostur-monath* (see the chapter on the Germanic Calendar). Both months were named after goddesses, who were each worshipped in their respective months. The name *Eostra* means "light rising up". The Indo-European word *aus* means "to shine". She was responsible for the morning light, the rising of the sun and the stars and for new life. Similar names are found for goddesses in Antiquity: Usatara (India), Aset Egypt) called Isis by the Greeks, Ishtar (Babylon), Astarte (Syria), Esther (Jews), Aurora (Latin), Ausrine (Latvia) and Ostara (Frisia).

The meaning of the name *Hreth* is uncertain. Some authors believe that *hreth* means "quick" and has to do with natural phenomena in February. I believe the word *hreth* is similar to the Danish word *ræd,* meaning "afraid, horrified". The old bird represents the mistress of the dead and she comes flying to collect the dying. Thus, she was probably called *Hreth* ("horrible").

Another interesting symbol on the purse is the man between two wolves – this will be addressed in a later chapter, entitled "the welcome symbol".

In AD 596, Pope Gregory the Great sent a delegation to England in order to Christianise the king of Kent. At that time, there were more than a dozen heathen kingdoms in England. These kingdoms had emerged through many battles between the Anglo Saxon groups and through the defeating of the Britons. In Anglo Saxon society, power was centralised in the royal family. Still the power of the king was not stable. He was not representing a single ethnic group as the earls once did. He was ruler of several ethnic groups. His heritage alone could not guarantee his legitimacy. His alliances could not be trusted. He could be threatened by rebels or assassins. The Christian missionary bishops offered the king legitimacy through their God. If the king introduced Christianity as the official religion of his Kingdom, he would be looked upon as chosen by God, by the church, by his subjects and by other Christian rulers: a divine kingship. In the old Germanic communities, the eril/earl was leader of the worship of the gods of the community. When the leader worshipped a new god, the common man would probably prepare himself for that. Consequently, the main interest of the first Christian missionary Bishops in England was converting the kings.

The best results of the mission were in Kent, south of Thames and Northumbria, probably because these areas had a considerable population of Britons and even a few surviving Christians. East Anglia and the Midlands took much longer. Mercia was the last kingdom to be Christianised.

In AD 731, Bede in his *Ecclesiastical History of the English People* writes about the introduction of Christianity into East Anglia. The missionary work was concentrated on the powerful kings:

> Edwin (King of Northumbria) was so zealous for the worship of truth, that he likewise persuaded Eorpwald (King of East Anglia), son of Redwald, to abandon his idolatrous superstitions, and with his whole province to receive the faith and sacraments of Christ. And, indeed, his father Redwald had long before been admitted to the sacrament of the Christian faith in Kent, but in vain; for on his return home, he was seduced by his wife and certain perverse teachers, and turned back from the sincerity of the faith; and thus his latter

state was worse than the former; so that, like the ancient Samaritans, he seemed at the same time to serve Christ and the gods whom he had served before; and in the same temple he had an altar to sacrifice to Christ, and another small one to offer victims to devils; which temple, Aldwulf, king of that same province, who lived in our time testifies had stood until his time, and that he had seen it when he was a boy. The aforesaid King Redwald was noble by birth, though ignoble in his actions. Eorpwald was, not long after he had embraced the Christian faith, slain by Richbert, a pagan; and from the time the province was under error for three years, till the crown came into the possession of Sigebert, brother to the same Eorpwald, a most Christian and learned man.

The Saxons

The Germanic tribes normally used spears as their weapon of choice. The word *German* means "spear men". The use of a spear does not demand much training. All men in the tribe could use it and actually did in the case of war. The word *Saxon* refers to the word *sachs* meaning "short sword" – to fight with a sword, more training is required. A sword could not be used by every man in the tribe; only by a minor warrior group. A short sword provides freedom of movement and is convenient for raids. Ambitious, young men in Germanic tribes obtained arms and training by joining warrior groups and partaking in war or plundering somewhere far away. As early as around AD 100, Tacitus mentioned companies of young Germanic warriors, who did not belong to a specific tribe. For a young man in a Germanic tribe, it was tempting to seek fame and fortune through plunder and piracy. Times were insecure. A tribe could be plundered by a warrior group from another tribe and the prisoners sold as slaves to the Romans. In those times, the formation of warrior groups was almost inevitable.

The "Saxones" are one of the Germanic tribes mentioned on Ptolemy's Map of AD 130. Ptolemy places them on the east bank of the River Elbe in modern Holstein. He identifies some islands in front of the inlet of River Elbe as "Saxon Islands". Tacitus does not mention the Saxons in his list of Germanic tribes from AD 100 AD. He situated the Reudigni tribe on the East bank of the Elbe. Many authors, myself included, believe that Ptolemy never placed Saxones on the map, but rather that the name he ascribed to that tribe has been misinterpreted by the many copyists, who were living in a time when the Saxons were well known. Indeed, one copyist wrote *Axiones* instead of Saxones.

In the land on the west bank of River Elbe, Ptolemy, as well as Tacitus, placed the Chauci tribe. This tribal name probably means "hackers" because they fought with axes. In the period AD 1-200, the culture of the people in this land was similar to the culture of the western parts of Schleswig and Holstein. They all resembled one another in their funeral fashions. Their urns were similar both in shape and ornamentation (Hodgkin 1952). These people, living near the North Sea, were called Ingvaeones by the Romans and they had the same god Ing.

The only written history of the old Saxons is by Widukind of Corvey in the AD 1000s. He wrote that people came over the Sea and took land in Haduloha and that there was a battle for the land. *Haduloha* is later known as Hadeln; Hadeln being the original name for the entire area between the rivers Elbe and Weser. Today, Hadeln is the name of a part of this area. However, this book uses the original *Haduloha* for the entire area.

Haduloha comprises the English word *hade,* meaning slope, rise and possible seaside, and the old German word *loh,* meaning clearing or meadow. The Indo-European *louko* means "open space". Thus, Haduloha could mean "seaside meadow". This is a good description of the landscape: a large part of it is (and was) marsh and there are little woods.

We know little about the invaders: they were a warrior group of the another tribe, but we do not know when they came or what they were called. In the second half of the AD 200s, inhumation burials appear on the west coast of southern Jutland and Holstein, which may be interpreted as the existence of a warrior class in this area. In the AD 400s, the Jutes had connections to Haduloha. We can assume that some people from Jutland or Holstein travelled by boat and attempted to take some land in Hadeln.

As there is no change in the material culture in Haduloha, we know that the Chauci tribe was not wiped out. The result of the invasion of a foreign warrior group could have been the establishment of a warrior class in Haduloha. But neither the written sources nor the archaeology indicate a princely ruler in Haduloha. It is more likely that further warrior groups established themselves in different parts of Haduloha. Some of them must have been former Chauci groups. Either way, the Chaucis probably originally emerged as an alliance of ethnic groups.

Haduloha had exceptionally many warrior graves – cremations as well as inhumations – from the last half of the AD 300s and from the AD 400s (Böhme 1974). The leading Germanic warrior families in Gaul and in Haduloha were rich as is evident in the splendid furnishings of the graves. The style and wealth of the equipment indicates that these warriors had served in the Roman army. In some of the graves, in the area between the Rhine and the Weser, were found coins distributed by rulers in Gaul in the first half of the AD 400s. These Roman rulers may have been usurpators, striving to be emperors in Rome. The coins suggest directly that the Germanic warriors were paid as mercenaries by these rulers (Böhme 1974). Saxons helping the Romans in wars against the Burgundies in AD 415 and 436 is mentioned earlier. Aetius, the ruler of Roman Gaul, we know had Saxons on his side when he defeated the Huns in AD 451.

The rich Germanic warrior graves in Haduloha indicate that these Germanic warriors were allied with Roman rulers. We may presume that Haduloha was divided into minor estates, each controlled by a warrior family or by a group of warriors. The different groups in Haduloha did not fight each other. There are no warlike signs at the settlements. The chieftains were independent and could go on raids by themselves anywhere but in Haduloha. They could also join each other and take part in wars as allies of Roman rulers. That is probably what happened in the few cases we know of, such as when we are told of Saxons fighting with the Roman army. From about AD 400, the people in Lower Saxony, including Haduloha, are called Saxon. Haduloha was the first Saxon land.

Lebuin was a missionary of the Saxons. He died in AD 776. *The Life of Lebuin* written in the AD 900s, describes the social organisation of the Saxons:

> In olden times, the Saxons had no king but appointed rulers over each village; and their custom was to hold a general meeting once a year in the centre of Saxony near the river Weser at a place called Marklo. There, all the leaders used to gather together and they were joined by twelve noblemen from each village with as many freedmen and serfs. There they confirmed the laws, gave judgement on outstanding cases and by common consent drew up plans for the coming year on which they could act either in peace or war.

Marklo means "demarcated meadow" and is now a village in Haduloha.

The Romans called the people near the sea *Chauci*. In AD 47, Chaucis and Frisians raided Gallia Belgica. In AD 170-200, Chauci raided on the Continent and in Britain. After AD 200, the Chauci are no longer mentioned as being in these coastal regions. The prevalent theory of the origin of the Saxons is that the Saxon tribe from the east conquered and drove away the tribes to west. But from the cemeteries with thousands of urns we know that this land still had a considerable population. They had almost the same beliefs as the Angles, which we can see from their urns. Nowell Myres, in his excellent book, *The English Settlements* (1986), concludes: "It would thus seem likely that the westward extension of Saxon power in the third century, while it broke up the old political hegemony of the Chauci, did not displace the bulk of the population". This statement allows for another theory: that in some tribes, like the Chauci, warrior groups emerged. These warriors were called Saxons.

Influenced from the East, more ethnic groups in both the Frisian areas and areas around the Rhine Mouth established warrior groups wielding swords. In the period AD 200-400, the ethnic groups lost their distinction and were replaced by "Saxons" in the reports. A warrior group would have the military power in the tribe and they probably exploited the resources in the tribe, but they earned their living as mercenaries or by plundering and piracy. As far as we know, Saxons did not raid other Saxons or Frisians. The warriors needed military adventures in order to obtain power and wealth, so they rowed their boats on the River Elbe and along the North Sea coast. Germanic boats were clinker built vessels, whereas the boats of the Roman provinces were carvel built. A clinker-built boat needs less internal framing and is lighter, faster and much easier to manoeuvre.

The spread of a warrior society is indicated by the emergence of inhumations. In the northern Netherlands, the dead were cremated until around AD 400. From that time onwards, cremations and inhumations were found side by side.

In the period AD 250-285, a number of forts were built on the Gallic and British coasts. The first recorded Saxon raid on these coasts was in the AD 280s. In AD 285, Carausius, a commander of Roman legions, was given the task of eliminating the Frankish and Saxon pirates. His mission was a successful one, but he was accused of being in league with the pirates and keeping their plunder for himself. He was condemned to death by the emperor of Rome, but Carausius declared himself emperor of an independent Britain and reigned until AD 293. In AD 370, seaborne Saxons called *Kouadoi*, interpreted as *Chauci*, settled in Batavia, an island in the Rhine Delta and from there, they drove away a Frankish tribe.

The priest and historian, Orosius, wrote in AD 416: "the Saxons are a people of the Ocean settled in pathless swamps and on the sea shore". Numerous mound-settlements have been found among the marshes that fringed the sea for most of the way from the Elbe to the Rhine. A typical excavated mound is Feddersen Wierde in Haduloha. The population on the mound increased in the AD 000s. In the AD 100s, a chieftain's house was built on the mound. This house is unusual in that it had no cattle-shed despite it having three barns. Related to the chieftain's house are some fifty houses including a bronze casting-house and a forge. The complex was – in contrast to the other houses on the mound – surrounded by a rampart with palisade. The fortified complex probably belonged to a warrior group. These people may have been called Saxons at some stage. Around AD 450, occupation of the site ended, probably due to migrating overseas to England. Pottery and other objects from the final phase correspond very closely with those found in settlements at Mucking, a site on the Thames estuary. Many settlements in Haduloha were abandoned in the AD 400s.

Many of the settlements and large urn fields along the North Sea coast area came to an end around AD 450. The number of finds decrease remarkably in the period AD 450-600. Pollen diagrams from Lower Saxony and Schleswig-Holstein also show a decrease in settlement indicators.

The East Saxons

In the period AD 100-500, the south coast of the Baltic Sea between the Elbe River and the Odra River was sparsely populated. What information we have about the Germanics in this area justifies calling them *East Saxons*. In this period, there was a change in their culture and religion. As we have seen, the original religious ideas of the Germanic tribes were similar to the ideas of the Angles. However, in times of migration, tribes had to change their social system and religion. Thus, warrior groups emerged in some tribes. These warrior groups frequently lived apart from their tribe, fighting as one for or against foreign warriors that may have had a more advanced culture. The rise of a new warrior culture was inevitable. Some East Saxon warrior groups adopted the ideas of Woden, Thunor and Freya. But how did these foreign religious ideas became part of the Germanic pantheon?

In AD 100, areas east of the Vistula River were dominated by the Sarmatians. Ptolemy called Eastern Europe *Sarmatia* and on his map we find the Sarmatian *Budini* tribe north of the source of the River Dnepr in modern Belarus. The letter *B* in the tribe name was probably pronounced as a *W*, but the Greek alphabet does not include a letter W. The Greek Ptolemy only had a *B* (soft b) for the W-sound. Around 400 BC, Herodotus placed the Budini at the Middle of River Dnepr. They were tall, blond, blue-eyed and light skinned. Their language was Scytian (Sarmatian). Alexander the Great called them Otena. The tribe name *Wudini* is derived from "Wu Din" meaning "victorious warrior" in both Sanskrit and Sarmatian. *Wu Din* was originally a title of a Sarmatian war-lord. The name Wu Din was changed to *Wotan* by the East Saxons, *Woden* by the Saxons in England and *Odin* by the Scandinavians.

The Sarmatian tribes were horse riders. Sarmatian culture included riding, military techniques, a chieftain caste, interment of the dead, burial mounds, grave stones, the sacrifice of horses, heavenly gods, precious jewellery, animal ornamentation and the high status of women. Moreover, their society had a warrior class that employed an advanced military technique.

There are reports of Sarmatian attacks on the Roman border but Sarmatian cavalry was equally used by the Roman army. Sarmatians had contact with Germanic tribes and they allied against the Roman Legions, but they were also rivals. For instance, the Roman emperor Maximin, who had a Gothik father and a Sarmatian mother, was the first non-Roman to become emperor in AD 235. Warriors with Sarmatian heritage were somehow adopted into some Germanic tribes where they became military leaders. Warfare and the influence of Sarmatian culture brought about a new social system in Germanic tribes. The warriors were tribal leaders and they became more powerful and superior to the rest of their own tribe, and their social contact with other leaders comprised of military cooperation,

Fig 28. Part of a Scythian drinking horn from Merdjany, Kuban, Russia, AD 200s BC

marriage, the educational residence of sons and precious gifts but to name a few.

A feature of Sarmatian religion is illustrated in figure 28. The mistress of life and death sits in heaven with her attributes: a tree of life and a horse skull. The horseman is a dead soul. He receives the drink of immortality in his horn from the bottle of the Goddess. After that he lives in the other world with the departed heroes.

The chieftain class in some Germanic tribes adopted aspects of Sarmatian culture including their religion. Germanic chieftains officiated as priests and the humbler classes of society normally accepted the beliefs of their superiors. The new gods resided in heaven and were called *Aesir* ("elevated").

The ancestor Woden was worshipped as a god but he also resided in heaven. When the worshippers of Woden died, their spirit went to heaven, where they received a seat at Woden's table according to their rank and reputation. They were not reborn as they would have been in traditional cyclical religion of the Germanics.

Being of noble descent was very important for the chieftain and warrior class because it legitimated their power. They believed that their powerful dead ancestors lived in another world and they practised ancestor worship. The idea of the living ancestor is related to interment burial. When the dead body of the person was buried with their personal belongings, the descendants could easily imagine that the dead person was a living spirit. Cremation, the traditional burial for the Germanics, implied on the other hand that the soul of the deceased had forgotten their previous life and was moving around in order to be reincarnated. These two principles are called salvation religion and cyclical religion, respectively. However, one kind of burial cannot always be equated with one kind of religion. For example, Christianity uses interment as well as cremation. The occurrence of isolated interment burials in Germanic cemeteries seems to spread from east to west, perhaps implying the rise of a new elite of chieftains and warriors in the Germanic tribes.

Samland is now Kaliningrad and lies near the outlet of the River Memel in the Baltic. The source of the River Memel is near to the source of the River Dnepr, where the Sarmatians lived. From the AD 000s, we see Sarmatian-style burials in Samland with burial mounds, rider outfit and horse sacrifices. The society in Samland is called Dolkheim-Kovrovo Culture (Nowakowski 1996). Here, we also have ordinary cremation burials, which means that the Sarmatian warrior class lived side-by-side with Baltic farmers. Artefacts produced in the Roman Empire are found in the graves, suggesting that Samland warriors partook in the Roman wars. Samland society is the first time we find a warrior elite living together with ordinary farmers in the Baltic Area. But in the centuries that follow, this kind of community spreads to the west.

Around AD 100, we see a similar culture, with horse sacrifices, in a Germanic tribe located at the outlet of the River Wistula. Around AD 275, the Greek Aithikos sailed around the European Continent (Wüttke 1853), and he noted that the River Oder was the border to the Saxons. At the outlet of the River Oder, he met a Germanic tribe

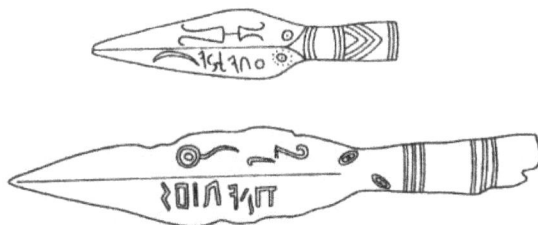

Fig 29. Sarmatian spearheads around AD 200 a) found in Dahmsdorf, near Berlin b) found in Kowel, northwest Ukraine (Shchukin 1994)

with a Sarmatian chieftain. He describes them as merchants, pirates and very good shipbuilders. Some early burial mounds and horse sacrifices have been found near the Oder outlet.

Ritual spearheads produced by Sarmates are decorated with the characteristic Sarmatian tamga symbol. The tamga is used as a heraldic symbol, but originally it symbolised a fire alter. A few of these spearheads have Germanic inscriptions in runes, such as in figure 29 where the inscription reads RANJA meaning "the runner". It may be the name of the spear. The inscription TILARIDS, on the other spearhead, means "target hitter" likewise probably the name of the spear. The two spearheads were likely produced for Germanic warriors, possible Saxons.

The Scythians (who were Sarmatians as well) had a very characteristic eagle symbol, probably a symbol of the mistress of

Fig 30. Buckle from Kossewen, Samland, around AD 200

heaven. For the Germanic farmers, the goddess of life and death resided primarily in the Earth. But for the Sarmatic or Germanic warrior groups, who were nomadic, the goddess had to be in heaven. And like the Valkyries of the Vikings, the heavenly goddess collected the souls of slain warriors and brought them to the realm of death. On the buckle from Samland in figure 30, we see the eagle sitting atop the world (*Museum für Vor- u. Frühgeschichte Berlin.*)

The war booty in Vimose ("sacred moor") in figure 31 belonged to an army from the south coast of the Baltic, which is from what I term the East Saxons. A similar eagle symbol has been found in Germanic princely graves, in Silesia, around AD 300, perhaps belonging to Vandals. In the AD 500s, we see the eagle symbol in Scandinavia, for instance on the island of Gotland and on the island of Funen (see the gold bracteate from Gudme in figure 85). Around AD 600, the eagle symbol came to England from Scandinavia, not via the Saxons (see the eagle from Sutton Hoo in figure 26).

The Icelandic historian Snorre provides a description of Odin's entry into the Germanic world in his *Prose Edda* (AD 1230):

> Odin made ready to journey out of Turkland, and was accompanied by a great multitude of people, young folk and old, men and women; and they had with them much goods of great price. And wherever they went over the lands of the earth, many glorious things were spoken of them, so that they were held more like gods than men. They made no end to their journeying till they were come north into the land that is now called Saxland; in that land Odin set up three of his sons for land-wardens. One was named Vegdeg: he was a mighty king and ruled over East Saxland; his son was Vitgils; his sons were Vitta, Hengest's father, and Sigarr, father of Svebdeg, whom we call Svipdagr. The second son of Odin was Beldeg, whom we call Baldr: he had the land which is

Fig 31. Wooden cup found in Vimose, on Funen, around AD 300

now called Westphalia. His son was Brandr, his son Frjódigar, (whom we call Fródi), his son Freóvin, his son Uvigg, his son Gevis (whom we call Gave). Odin's third son...

The genealogy from the royal house of Kent includes the sequence Woden—Witta—Withgils–Hengist, a sequence recognisable in the four names of Snorre's list. In the genealogy of the West Saxons (Wessex), we find this sequence of kings: Woden—Baeldaeg—Brand—Freothogar—Freawin—Wig—Gewis. These seven names are the same as those given by Snorre. Perhaps because Snorre from Iceland had knowledge of old Anglo-Saxon manuscripts, written by monks. Anglo-Saxon monks tried to keep track of politics, i.e., the line of kings in England and their ancestors, even from before they settled in England. *Woden* is the title of a victorious chieftain and any Saxon family could claim to have an ancestor with this title.

New religious practices could only be introduced to a tribe by a person with knowledge of that practice and who resided in the tribe. We do not know exactly how foreigners ended up in this position, but some old legends may provide some insight. For instance, *The Danish History, Book III* (Saxo) contains some essential information regarding Balder. Balder lived in the last half of the AD 200s, and he wanted to marry a princess from a kingdom in southern Jutland and conquer her kingdom. This kingdom may have been in Ellem Syssel (figure 6), where the village of Bolderslev, is said to be where Balder died. He attacked Hother, who was engaged to the princess. Hother was a Hadbard, who gave his name to the town of Haderslev in Barwith Syssel.

One of their battles was a naval one. Balder said he was descended from the gods and had Odin and Thor on his side. Conversely, Hother was helped by the three norns, who gave him a magic coat of mail. Hother won the battle and Balder fled. Gelder, the King of Saxony, who met his end in the same war, was laid upon the corpses of his oarsmen by Hother, and then placed on a pyre built of vessels. This battle probably relates to a sacrifice of war booty in Ejsbøl Moor, near Haderslev, from around AD 275. Here, iron spikes from a burned ship, a precious golden belt and weapons from 200 men were found. The find may represent the belongings of the Saxon king, Gelder. Hother and Balder continued to face each other in battle and Balder even acquired the princess and her kingdom for a while. In the last battle, Balder was fatally wounded by Hother. In Neudorf-Bornstein, in southeastern Istathe Syssel, a rich grave with a precious belt similar to the belt in Eisbøl was found. This may be Balder's grave.

Indeed, a lot of stories regarding the death of Balder, Odin's son, have survived in Norse Mythology, probably kept alive by the Saxons of Balder's lineage. But the worship of Odin did not continue in southern Jutland, though it was revived in the Viking Age.

Essentially, the East Saxons typically formed professional warrior groups. Their means of transport were well build rowing boats or horses, and they adopted some Sarmatian traditions and religious ideas. The warrior groups could be rulers in the local tribe, and they were often allied to other warrior groups, sometimes with familial connections. Warrior groups came from different tribes, but they sometimes worked together as a unit called *Saxon*. In AD 260, the three units: Saxons, Alemannis and Franks broke through the border of the Roman Empire, conquering southern Germany and moving the border south.

Hengist invaded Kent with some Jutish warriors but, according to the genealogy of the royal house of Kent, he was a descendant of Witta. Witta is mentioned in the Old English poem *Widsith*, the most reliable description of Germanic tribes in the AD 400s. It says "Witta weold Swæfum" – [The Swæfum that Witta ruled], probably lived near the contemporary city Schwerin, 100 km east of Hamburg. Several place names featuring *Witte* are found in this neighbourhood. In addition, there are villages called Wotenitz, Wotenick and Wotrum named after Wotan, and Jassewitz named after the Aesir, the heavenly gods. We may call the Swæfum tribe East Saxons as Snorri called this part East Saxland. Personal names and place names indicate that the Swæfum had a chieftain class that had adopted the Aesir gods from the Sarmatians around AD 400. Hengist probably belonged to this East Saxon tradition. From Schwerin, you can paddle down a tributary of the Elbe, down the Elbe itself and out to Haduloha (later, suggestions that Haduloha was populated by Saxon warrior groups from the different tribes of the Chaucis, Jutes, Swæfum and probably more in AD 300s will be addressed). Haduloha was a wealthy stronghold of the Saxon warlords, and the Saxons found here had probably developed ideas of Odin and Thunor. In the middle of Haduloha, we find the place name Odisheim probably named after Odin/ Wodin.

The area between the Elbe and Rhine, including Haduloha, is called Lower Saxony and Westphalia. The population here seems to have enjoyed a common pagan culture in the period AD 400-800.

They are referred to as Old Saxons. They also embraced some east Saxon ideas such as the independent warrior groups. As we have seen, the warrior elite seems to have been influenced by Sarmatic culture, and they worshipped the ancestral god Wotan. Warrior graves with horse burials have been found. In the Saxon cemetery in Liebenau, on the west bank of the River Weser, were some horse burials. The oldest is dated to around AD 500 (Hässler 1983). In AD 800, the Old Saxons were eventually subdued by the Frankish king Charlemagne and, ultimately, forced to convert to Christianity. Saxons were compelled to answer the question: "Do you renounce Wodan, Thunor, Saxnot and all other monsters?" (Saxnot is well known from other texts. He was probably Tiw, the supreme Germanic god).

The Saxon Emigration

The Saxons were not a tribe located somewhere at the North Sea Coast. They were warrior groups with members from one or from different tribes. Much effort has been made to determine the material and spiritual culture of Saxons, where it originated and where it emerged in England.

The equal-armed brooch was common in Haduloha in the AD 400s, and as it is almost only found in Haduloha, it must have been produced there. This brooch was made by a technique called chip-carving, a technique first found by Germanics in Roman service. We may assume that some Germanic craftsmen moved from the Roman area to the Germanic one, thus the brooch is considered Saxon. Some of the women, who wore this brooch, were married to Saxon warriors in Haduloha. A few equal-armed brooches have been found in the Anglian areas in Middle England, having been brought there by female immigrants arriving via the Ouse River and the Fens. These women may also have been Angles from southern Jutland, staying for a short while in Haduloha.

The brooches pictured in figure 32 are gilded. They belonged to an inhumation burial in an old bronze-age mound in Haduloha.

Fig 32. Equal-armed brooch and two eagle brooches from a grave in Ander-lingen, Haduloha, AD 400s (Hässler 1991)

Equal-armed brooches are always found on their own. They were worn on the chest to hold a cape. Most Germanic ornaments have a spiritual meaning, so the same can be assumed of this brooch, with the two almost symmetrical parts representing the upper and the lower worlds, heaven and earth, respectively. More or less the same idea in found in the cruciform and square-headed brooches. On the bridge between the two worlds in figure 32 is a stylised figure that may be explained as a human soul flying towards heaven. Oppositely placed animals are found in both worlds – perhaps representing all living creatures.

The two small brooches were worn on the shoulders to hold a dress. As noted earlier, the mythical eagle represents the mistress of heaven (see figures 26, 30, 31 and 85). It is interesting that the eagle carries a human mask just like the eagle from Sutton Hoo in figure 26. The mask represents a dead soul being carried away by the heavenly mother.

In the second half of the AD 300s, some Germanic warriors settled in Gaul. The Roman army in northern France and Belgium was composed of Germanic mercenaries. Böhme has studied more than 100 Germanic graves in the area between the Rhine and the Seine. Most of them included weapons and were male graves. These Germanic warriors were well paid by the rulers in Gaul; some of them even seem to have been landowners (Böhme 1974). The brooches and hairpins in the female graves followed the same fashion as those graves east of the Rhine, which means that the Germanic warrior families in Gaul came from the Germanic area now called Lower Saxony (especially Haduloha). After AD 400, the fashion pertaining to the various areas developed independently of each other, indicating that the migration of Germanic warriors into Gaul decreased.

Fig 33. Bronze strap ends from Abbeville by the River Somme, AD 400s (Salin 1904)

In the second half of the AD 400s, some of the Germanic warriors from Gaul invaded the south coast of England. Germanic cemeteries south of the Thames are composed of inhumation burials, and if there cremation burials are present in a cemetery, they are only a minority. Men's graves included weapons and bronze buckles; women's graves included brooches and girdle hangers. Evison has shown that some of these artefacts were produced in northern Gaul near the River Somme, and production continued in England for a few decades (Evison 1965).

Many of the bronze artefacts have ornaments similar to those in figure 33. Here, we see two mythical animals facing a mask in the centre-point. The two animals probably represent the Divine Twins, the most popular deities of the Germanics during the period of the great migrations. The mask probably represents the goddess of light, appearing as the Dawn. As we have seen, Bede records that the

111

Fig 34. Decoration on a brooch from Canterbury, Kent

Angles in England called her Eostra meaning "raising light" and she was worshipped by many nations during Antiquity. It is noteworthy that the bronze founding technique was first used in the Roman provinces but the ornamentation is Germanic. The interpretation of the symbols will be explained elsewhere.

The same style and almost the same motive is seen on the brooch from Canterbury in figure 34, but here the mask looks like a man. There is also a man's face on the buckle from Galsted in figure 19. Most likely the Divine Twins guiding the rebirth of the man. The prone face on the buckle may represent the dead man before his rebirth.

Gildas, a British priest writing around AD 540, says that that an appeal for help was sent from the ruler of Roman Britain to Aetius, ruler of Roman Gaul. When the Huns were defeated in AD 451, Childeric became king of the Franks and ruled the Roman province of

Belgium. From there, he fought Saxons, Alemannis and Goths. The fighting with the Franks may have caused Saxon warriors in Gaul to migrate to rich southern England, where they had good chances as the first Germanic kingdom had just been established by Hengist in Kent.

The burials south of Thames indicate an invasion of warrior families from northern Gaul in the second half of the AD 400s. The Germanics themselves did not keep written records so, as of yet, there is no way to know what the invaders called themselves. Some contemporary authors refer to them as "Franks" because they came from northern Gaul. *Franks* was a collective name for several ethnic groups, who abandoned maritime expeditions and settled inland. Neither do we know what the Germanic warriors who arrived from Gaul called themselves. Native Briton writers called them Saxons thus that is the term used here. The Romans and the Britons called all the Germanic people in Britain "Saxons". In Christian times, Anglian clerks used the Latin word *Saxonia* for the Germanic part of Britain and the word *Angelcyn* for the Germanics in England and *Englisc* for the language. Indeed, the word *Saxon* was political rather than ethnic.

In Sussex, the first Germanic finds from the second half of the AD 400s are concentrated in an area near Brighton, where Romano-British settlement had been sparse. Germanic cemeteries have been found 20 km east of Brighton and 20 km west of Brighton at the stronghold of Highdown. The Saxon conquest of Sussex is described in the Anglo-Saxon Chronicle for AD 477. The time needs to be reconciled as the years in the Chronicle appear to be 20 years too late.

AD 457 (reconciled time): "Ælle landed in Britain and his three sons – Cymen and Wlencing and Cissa – with three ships, at the place which is called Cymenes ora; and there they slew many of the Welsh and some that [fled] they drove into the wood that is called Andredesleage".

And in AD 471 (reconciled time): "Ælle and Cissa besieged the stronghold of Anderida and slew all that were therein, nor was one Briton left there afterwards".

The name *Ælle* means "the high one". He and his Saxon warriors probably came from Gaul. Ælle founded a kingdom in Sussex – the second Germanic kingdom in Britain after Kent.

In the AD 400s, there was also a migration to England from the coastal areas between the Elbe and the Rhine rivers. Some authors refer to the people in these areas as Saxon because Saxon warrior groups came from there. However, the inhabitants were, in general, not called Saxons. Furthermore, the immigrants from there settled all over England; not just in the so-called Saxon areas south of the Thames, as evident from the spread of the use of saucer brooches from this area into England. Female graves demonstrate that a pair of saucer brooches were used to hold up a dress, one at each shoulder. The distribution of these brooches in England should not have been used as a mark of a Saxon invasion in England, because saucer brooches are spread both north and south of the Thames.

Actually, many immigrants came from the Frisian area. The East Roman historian Procopius, writing around AD 550, reported that in his day the population of Britain, apart from native Britons, was divided between Angles and Frisians.

Applied saucer brooches were made of two separate circular plates of bronze. The decorated and stamped plate was fixed onto a plain metal back plate, which ranged in diameter from 2 to 8 cm. These brooches were used by Germanics as early as the AD 200s at the

Upper Elbe, modern Czech Republic. The Germanics here were called *Marcomanni*. Around AD 260, several Germanic allies attacked the Roman border: Alamannies, Saxons, Franks as well as Marcomannies. Saucer brooches then became fashionable and spread to the Lower Elbe and the Weser and the Rhine. There is a later variant where the entire brooch is cast in one piece and produced using chip-carving. During the first half of the AD 400s, both types spread into England and their use stopped on the Continent. Most of the saucer brooches in England were produced locally but the fashion must have been brought by migrants. These brooches were very popular in England in the AD 500s.

Most saucer brooches have geometric designs such as concentric circles, stars, crosses, scrolls or masks. The meaning of these motifs is not clear, but it would be a mistake to explain them as mere decoration. The Germanics had no written language; rather, they used figurative language to express their ideas. Most Germanic decorations contain – as we have seen – a spiritual meaning. Indeed, ornamentation was personal and slightly different on each specimen, but it is possible to offer an understanding of such decoration:

Concentric circles: often symbols of the shining Sun. If this interpretation is accepted and Germanic deities related to the Sun are sought, then picture symbols such as the strap ends in figure 33 is worth considering, on which the raising of the goddess Eostra ("raising light") is featured. She was probably responsible for the rising Sun. Thus, implying that the designs are symbols of the goddess of light.

By the lower Rhine River, 150 alters from around AD 200, have been found with inscriptions such as *Matronae Austriahenae*. The area near Cologne was controlled by the Romanised Ubii tribe. In this area, alters with the three matrones were built by different ethnic groups. The inscription probably means "Matronae for the Austrians", suggesting that the name of the goddess of delivery was something like *Austria* – at least for some of the Germanic tribes.

Unfortunately, there is no written records of the Germanic gods. In the Edda poem *Sigrdrífumál* ("sayings of the victory-bringer"), we have an invocation to the gods. The Valkyrie, Sigrdriva, offers a full horn of mead to Sigurd and gives a speech beginning in stanza 2.

Hail, Day! Hail, sons of Day!
Hail Night and her daughter now!
Look on us here with loving eyes,
That waiting we victory win.

This fragment is the only direct invocation of the Norse gods, which has been preserved, and it is sometimes dubbed a "pagan prayer". Day is the god of heaven (Tiw). The sons of Day are the Divine Twins. Night is the mother of gods (Hretha) and her daughter is the Dawn (Eostra). This myth is similar to other ancient myths from India, Greece and the Baltic countries.

Stars: some saucer brooches are decorated with star, probably

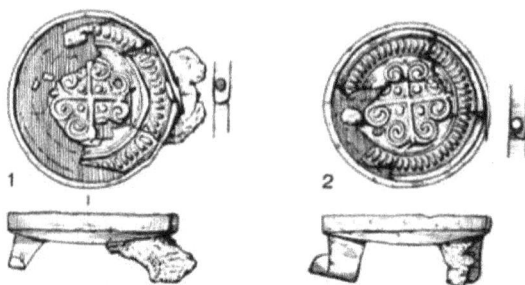

Fig 35. Pair of ornamented saucer brooches from a grave in Great Chester-ford, Essex around AD 450 (Evison 1994)

representing a heavenly deity. In some Edda poems, one of the Divine Twins, Frey, appears as the Morning Star.

Crosses: saucer brooches with a cross decoration have been found near the Elbe River and in England (figure 35). The circle cross is a very old and widespread symbol used throughout Europe since the Neolithic and was even used in the Nordic Bronze Age. It is sometimes called a sun cross, but the sun has no cross. The circle cross is probably a worldwide symbol for the spiritual world or heaven. All prehistoric people believed in the spiritual world. The arms represent the four directions of the world and the circle is the end, the horizon. There is nothing else in this symbol, because the spiritual world is invisible. According to the New Testament, Jesus was fixed to a pole, *stauros*. In the AD 200s, the Christian Church condemned the cross because it was pagan. The first time we see the use of the cross in the Christian Church is in middle of the AD 400s, when it was used on a sarcophagus in the Vatican, and even then it was an equal-armed cross, meaning the spiritual world, Heaven. The Germanics used the circle cross in the same way; thus it can be assumed that the brooch with the cross was an adoration of

Fig 36. Saucer brooches from North Wessex: a) East Shefford; b) Colling-bourne Ducis (British Museum)

the heavenly gods.

Many of the saucer brooches with crosses have scrolls such as the one in figure 35. Scrolls are decorative elements, but they are also symbols of force and energy, representing invisible forces. Together with the heavenly cross, scrolls may represent natural forces, coming from abroad.

Scrolls: another common decorative feature was scrolls, spirals in a row (figure 36a, called a "meander" in classical archaeology and a "running dog" in Nordic archaeology. Besides being a decoration, it is a symbol of the movement of time (see the short horn figure 57). The inward moving spiral represents night and the outward moving spiral represents day. Therefore, the decoration may be an adoration of the gods of day and night. Another interpretation is that the inward moving spiral represents the death of a human being and the outward moving spiral represents a new life (see the chapter entitled *The Human Life Cycle*).

The early applied saucer brooches in England are distributed both north and south of the Thames with the exception of a concentration in the Upper Thames area. Here, all the brooches with spirals in a row are found, indicating a Germanic settlement at the Upper Thames in the first half of the AD 400s. The settlers followed the river (Evison 1978).

Masks: as seen in figure 36b. Most likely it is the dawn, Eostra. Compare the monster on the sceattas in figure 25 and the mask in figure 36b.

As we have noted, the majority of the Germanic people that migrated to England were small ethnic communities. In some cases, entire communities left their old homelands accompanied by their leaders. These ethnic groups were not one great Anglian tribe, but they were called *Angles* in England because they believed in the same god Ing. The name *Angle* is cultural rather than ethnic. The Saxon invaders were more advanced. They had a leading class of nobles and warriors. However, the warrior groups did not represent an ethnic community – they set out for England with whatever daredevils they could find. The Saxons organised a hierarchy and, after a while, established small kingdoms in the areas south of the Thames Valley. East Anglian and Middle English dialects seem to have some vocabulary in common with old Norse, which is not shared with West Saxon or Kentish.

The Anglian settlements north of the Thames and all the lands around the Fens have large cremation cemeteries. In Kent and all the regions south of the Thames, the situation in the second half of the AD 400s seems to have taken a radically different form. Common to all southern areas is the complete absence of large cremation cemeteries, and where cremation does occur, it comprises a

Fig 37. Disc brooch from Kingston, Kent, around AD 600

comparatively minor component in cemeteries that consist predominantly of inhumation burials (Myres 1986). The inhumation burials probably belong mostly to the British population and to the invading Saxon warrior elite to some extent.

The saucer brooches became popular in England in the AD 500s and the beginning of the AD 600s. They are also called disc brooches and the smaller ones (2 cm), button brooches. The pre-Christian Germanics in Kent produced elaborate disc brooches with a circle cross. In a woman's grave from the AD 500s, a gold brooch with inlaid jewels was found (figure 37). Underneath a large burial mound was a huge grave containing a sturdy coffin with the skeleton of a small woman wearing the brooch. It is made of gold with settings of jewels, blue glass and shell. The brooch was produced in Kent probably around AD 600, but the use of inlaid jewels points to the Sarmatian jewellery tradition. This style was adopted by some of the Germanic warrior elite, for instance the Frankish rulers. It is probable that some of the Saxons from Gaul who settled in Kent were goldsmiths. Some of the ornaments on the brooch are similar to the distorted animals on the strap ends in figure 33.

The Jutes

According to Bede, Jutes settled in Kent and on the Isle of Wight. The urns found in Kent resemble urns from Jutland (Myres 1986), strongly implying that some of the settlers in Kent were Jutes. According to *The Anglo-Saxon Chronicle*, Hengist and his brother Horsa came to Kent AD 449. But it is vital to note that the years calculated in the *Chronicle* are off by 20 years (Ahrens 1978). Hengist arrived in AD 430 with Jutish warriors in order to help the British commander Vortigern fight against the Picts. Around AD 540, the British monk Gildas wrote the treatise *On the Ruin and Conquest of Britain* – the only written source from the time of the conquest. According to Gildas, a small group came and settled there first. He states that they came in three *cyulis* (or "keels"), "as they call ships of war". This small group invited more of their countrymen to join them, and the settlement grew. Eventually, the Saxons demanded that "their monthly allotments" be increased and, when their demands were eventually refused, they broke the treaty and plundered the lands of the Romano-British". Gildas describes how their raids took them

> sea to sea, heaped up by the eastern band of impious men; and as it devastated all the neighbouring cities and lands, did not cease after it had been kindled, until it burnt nearly the whole surface of the island, and licked the western ocean with its red and savage tongue. The Britons endured the horrors of pitiless raids and left behind them tracks of unburied corpses and ruined towers.

The revolt occurred around AD 442. Vortigern then had to give the Jutes land in eastern Kent, including the town of Canterbury. A cemetery with cremations – probably from the Jutish invaders – has been found in Canterbury, which was the administration centre of the Roman district of Kent. Indeed, elements of this administration were probably still in existence when Hengist and his men took over. They kept up some of these administration systems and used Canterbury as a royal seat. However, Germanics and Romans had different methods of administration. The Romans collected taxes from farmers, mostly in the form of grain. These taxes were then used for civil administration and the army. Germanic kings, on the other hand, let the farmers grow what they liked and animal husbandry was common. Instead, the king demanded active service from farmers. Even the king's housecarls could have their own estates – a great landowner might have many warriors to feed and was called "lord", originally "hlaford" ("bread keeper").

Hengist and his men were professional warriors with international political experience. They probably came from Haduloha, where, as we have seen, there was a mixture of ethnic Germanic groups. Hengist and his son Aesc established the first Germanic kingdom in Britain quite quickly. More Germanic warriors were welcomed and they subsequently conquered more land. Vortigern and other British commanders had to surrender Kent, Sussex, south Wessex and the Isle of Wight. The Britons were confused and had no trained army. In the 25 years after the revolt, the number of Germanic migrants coming up the Thames was considerable. Some of them were Saxon warriors from Haduloha or Gaul.

The Huns were defeated in a great battle in AD 451 and many Germanic warriors had to find a new battleground. But most of the migrants were populations from the coastal areas of the North Sea. The Kentish king also controlled Essex, thereby controlling the traffic of migrants on the Thames.

A figure named Hengest, who might be identifiable as the Hengist of the *Chronicle* and Hengest in the genealogy from the royal house of

Kent, appears in *Beowulf*. A song was recited in king Hrothgar's hall. It mentioned King Hnæf, son of King Hoc. Hnæf was allied to Hrothgar and they were both referred to as West Danes. But they were also Jutes. Hnæf's family, the Hockings, were probably neighbours to Barwith Syssel at the North Sea. Here, we have the place names Oksbøl, Ho Bay and Nebel. Hnæf's sister Hildeburg was married to the Frisian king, Finn Folkwalda. Folkwalda means that he was the ruler of several warrior groups who lived in Friesland.

Hnæf and Finn met in a battle at sea, where Hnæf's sons were killed. Then Hnæf travelled with some allies to Finn's castle in order to be compensated. Among the allies were some *eutenum* such as Hunlaf, Oslaf and Guthlaf. In the *Skjoldnunga Saga*, chapter IV, mention is made of a king of Denmark named Leifus who had six sons, three of whom are named Hunleifus, Oddleifus and Gunnleifus, which corresponds exactly to these three allies. Some authors believe that *eutenum* means "giants" (stemming from *jötunn* and *eóten*), whereas others, myself included, believe it means "Jutes". Nevertheless, the guests were welcomed and Hnæf and the other guests received valuable presents and peace agreements. The famous sword fighter Hengest was also among Hnæf's allies. Hengist was given one of Finn's two castles in Friesland. The guests stayed overnight. That night they were ruthlessly attacked by Finn's warriors. The fighting went on for five days and many were killed on both sides, among them Hnæf. Finn had to give up the fight. When the battle was over, the dead were cremated in a large pyre. Some of the surviving guests chose to stay through the winter and Finn took care of them. In the spring, Hengist and the other guests slayed Finn and his warriors and confiscated all the values in the castle.

The drama in Finn's castle tells us that Hengist became a powerful warlord in Friesland and that he was allied with Jutish chieftains and that some of his warriors were Jutes. This explains why he is said to be leader of a Jutish invasion in Kent. According to the genealogy from the house of Kent, Hengist had a follower, Octa, as a king of Kent. The name *Octa* suggests he belonged to the Jutish chieftain family of Hockings.

Several Saxon expeditions came from Haduloha and Jutes seem to have participated in some of them. In AD 534, the Frankish king Teutebert send a letter to Emperor Justinian saying that the kingdom of Thüringians had disappeared and that the "Saxon Jutes" had now subjugated to the Frankish kingdom.

Finn's castles were in Friesland in the first half of the AD 400s. In this period, there were many warrior graves in Haduloha and several precious metal objects, such as that in figure 32, were produced. Perhaps warlord Hengist had his seat in Haduloha. Hengist probably came from a chieftain family, the Swefs, located near Schwerin. They were able to reach Haduloha by boat. Moreover, it is reasonable that the Jutes picked up Hengist from Haduloha on their way to Friesland. The drama ended with Hengist seizing complete power.

Another piece of evidence, which suggests Hengist was in Haduloha is the local myth of *Hengist and Horsa*. In what is now Lower Saxony and Holstein, horse head gables, or gable signs adorned with two rampant horse figures, were referred to as "Hengst and Hors" up until the late 1800s (figure 39). Quite plausibly, we have a tradition here dating back to the Germanic worship of the Divine Twins.

Furthermore, it indicated that the Divine Twins were worshipped and depicted as two horses by the Saxons before their invasion of England. This ornamentation tradition has survived in the Saxon Homelands but, unfortunately, the deeper meaning is now lost.

A Frisian myth tells of a young girl named Swana, a great-grandchild

Fig 39. Gable decorations in Lower Saxony and Holstein called "Hengst and Hors", 1800s

of Woden, who had two brothers, Hengist and Horsa, who were killed. Later, she was married to the duke of Friesland, Udolphus (same name as Hrothulf) and had two sons, whom she called Hengist and Horsa in memory of her brothers. These sons became the famous brothers who directed the invasion of Britain. This myth is an adaptation of the widely distributed myth of the Divine Twins. For instance, the Roman twins Castor and Pollux were born from an egg from the swan Leda. Being a god, Leda could be both mother and sister to the Divine Twins and Frisian Swana has a similar capacity.

The ancestors of many Germanic tribes were a pair of brothers (this is further elaborated in the chapter entitled "The two Warriors"). However, it is likely that the myth of the Divine Twins, Hengist and Horsa, as leaders of the invasion of Kent is a later construction. Hengist was the brave and strong twin, naturally revered by the warrior class. Likewise, Castor was the most venerated twin by the Romans. On the other hand, the Saxon warlord in the chronicles was called Hengist. He was considered a mortal incarnation of the Divine

Twin. Hengist also worshipped his ancestor god Woden and his Jutish Warriors probably adopted that worship.

29 bracteates have been found in Kent, demonstrating a connection to Jutland. They are all of the type D (the typical example in figure 40b). These bracteates were produced, at first, around AD 550 in considerable numbers in an area in Mid-Jutland and another area in southern Jutland. Later, the type D was produced in Kent, in Haduloha and in south-eastern Norway – clearly as a consequence of migration. The migration of the Jutes after AD 550 is one of the last migrations into England. These Jutes chose Kent because they had relationship with the Jutes living in Kent since Hengist's time. Some Jutes migrated to Haduloha, where Jutes held strong positions.

The figure on the bracteates in figure 40 has the head of a bird of prey. Follow the body: the shoulder is a bow and from it extends a leg. The next bow is the hip and then the other leg. The mythical creature is entangled in itself and looks under control. Creatures on D-bracteates are often accompanied by two small symbols: a pretzel and a leg. The pretzel symbol is known from the Bronze Age and is assumed to mean human life from conception to death. It's possible

Fig 40. D-bracteates. a) from Grathe Hede, Jutland (Hauck cat. 434b,1) and b) from Finglesham, Kent (Hauck cat. 426,2b)

the leg means feasibility – but it is uncertain.

The brooches found in Kent demonstrate a connection to Jutland. Sonia Chadwick in a study of the Anglo-Saxon cemetery at Finglesham, Kent stated that "the Jutish Style B brooches in Kent are best explained by the presence in Kent of a craftsman from Jutland". The serpent like creature is probably the creature known in Scandinavia as a *Lindworm* (meaning "pliable worm"). In England, the same creature is called a *Wyvern*. Other Germanic people have the similar Dragon, although the dragon usually has two more legs (four in total). In Scandinavia, there are much local folklore about a *Lindworm*: it can protect people but it can also terrorise people and demand human lives. It can even spit "venom", what we nowadays would call infection. Most stories relate to a Lindworm trying to prevent the building of a church. The Lindworm is invisible and can fly, but lives mostly in water or underground. The serpent-like creature in the underworld is an old idea of the Germanic people, as we will see later.

The Lindworm, Wyvern and Dragon are all connected by envy, famine, war and epidemics. All these plagues emerged a few years after the climate catastrophe of AD 540. In southern Scandinavia, famine was followed by fighting, plundering and probably epidemics. In England, a severe plague was reported in around AD 549.

Amulets may not be capable of influencing the behaviour of the gods, but they are capable of influencing the faithful people who wear them. In times of need, trouble, insecurity or danger people become more religious. Faith gives confidence, patience and courage – particularly, when such faith and rituals are shared in a group. The faithful did not panic easily as a result of the famine.

In times of famine, many people fought over resources. Robbing and killing became normal. The old systems of power were replaced with new ones. In Scandinavia, many settlements were attacked and burned. This also happened to the last Danish Scylding king Hrothulf (the Danish Rolf Krake) around AD 550 in Lejre on Sealand. Snorre, who wrote about the Scandinavian kings says:

> Östen, Adils son, then ruled over the Sveer. In his days fell Rolf Krake in Leire. At this time, warlords wasted much in Sweden, Danes as well as Norwegians. Many were seakings, who had a great army but did not own any land. Only the one could be a truly seaking who never slept under sooted purlin and never drinked beside the fireplace.

The Danish central power disappeared and the production of gold bracteates came to an end with the exception of the D-type, which took over in the last period of the gold bracteates. The D-bracteates may be understood as protection against injury from a monster. The amulet shows respect for the monster but as the legs are entangled, the monster is quiet, ensuring the safety of the person wearing the amulet.

Beowulf provides an example of how infectious diseases and epidemics were explained in the AD 500s: one of Beowulf's warriors stole a valuable drinking cup from a burial mound that was guarded by a dragon. The dragon became angry and in line 2313:

Then the demon began to spew flames,
To burn bright houses; the gleam of fire rose
To the horror of the men; nor there anything alive
The hateful air-flier wished to leave
The war-strength of that wyrm was widely seen,
The malice of the darkly cunning one near and far.

Beowulf is hurt by the dragon, but he is able to take part in the mysterious killing of a stranger. But then Beowulf's illness erupts in line 2711:

Then the wound began,
Which him the earth-dragon had caused earlier,
To swelter and to swell; he soon discovered that
It him in the breast welled with deadly evil,
Poison inside.

Beowulf then states his dying wish.

The Aesir Gods

In a description from AD 600 of the life of Saint Kentigern, patron saint of Glasgow, it is said that the Angles believed that Woden was their ancestor and worshipped him, but that Woden was a mortal human being and a king of the Saxons. Some Anglo-Saxon royal houses considered Woden to be an important ancestor. However, there is little indication of Woden being worshipped among the Anglo Saxon population in England. Only in Kent do we have archaeological evidence from the AD 500s suggesting the worship of Woden. The place name Woodnesborough means "Woden's Hill". Here, a grave containing sacrificed horses and a one-eyed weapon-dancer, both characteristic of the Woden cult, were found.

Furthermore, in nearby Ash, another grave held an amulet in the form of Thunor's hammer and some gold-bracteates. Woodnesborough and Ash are close to Sandvich, where Hengist probably landed. In Kent, we also have the place name Wye meaning "sanctuary". In a woman's grave in Kingston, Kent from the AD 500s a gold brooch with inlaid jewels was found (see figure 37). It is in the form of a circular cross, which normally symbolises heaven. In Kent, we also find Thunores hlaew ("Thor's Mound").

Some Saxon warriors brought a new family of gods to England, the Aesir family. The most prominent members were Woden and Thunor. The word *Aesir* means "lord". It comes from the Indo-European *asura*, found in other Indo-European languages as sire, sir, zar and shah all meaning "lord". The original meaning of *asura* was probably "high, raised". In fact, the strongest characteristic of the Aesir is that they live above, in heaven. They are invisible as they live in the spiritual world. The traditional Germanic gods, the Vanir, on the other hand, lived everywhere: above, on and below the Earth and even in living beings. The most prominent Vanir ("fair, beautiful") were Mother Earth and the Divine Twins.

Hengist was probably related to the Swef tribe, who regarded Woden as their ancestor. Hengist and his Jutish followers, who became the leading class in Kent, had faith in Woden because he could help them. Ancestor worshippers believe that the souls of their ancestors live in another world, which occupies the same space as the world of the living beings, but are normally invisible to us. The spirits from the spiritual world had the power to influence the souls and minds of living beings, other dead spirits and even the gods. Woden was the most powerful in the spiritual world and could be a great help to his descendants. In war, he could give his supporters courage and spread confusion among the enemies. Indeed, Woden was a war god; he urged his followers to start wars in order to slay other rulers. The dead souls of slain rulers would then be obedient to Woden, strengthening his power in the spiritual world. Furthermore, the worshippers of Woden were promised a splendid life after death in

Fig 41. Bronze amulet in the form of a hammer from a grave in the Saxon cemetery at Ash, Kent (AD 500s)

the company of Woden and his supporters.

The Saxon thunder god *Thunor* can probably be traced back to the Sarmatic thunder god *Targitai*. His name is a compound of *tar*, meaning "protection" and *gitai*, meaning "giver". Targitai had two bucks just like Thunor had. *Thunor* is Germanic and refers to thunder. The Saxons presumably had a thunder god and Thunor just assumed some of the properties of the Sarmatian thunder god. Thunor had power over storms and lightning. He could fight the vicious elements by throwing his hammer again and again because the hammer always returned to him. The amulet from Kent (figure 41) presumably represents the hammer of the thunder god. However, looking closer, it seems the head of the hammer resembles a bird or the head of a goat. It is decorated with circles with a marked centre – this symbol is old. As we have seen, the circle is a symbol for the sky, possibly symbolising the shining sky with the

Fig 42. The belt buckle from Finglesham, Kent, around AD 600

sun, which is significant given that the god of thunder resides in the sky.

In a grave in Finglesham, near Sandwich in Kent, a belt buckle of gilded bronze was found (figure 42). The three "knobs" may be indicative of a local tradition in Kent; corresponding to the three forces of life as on the brooches in figure 23. On the other hand, the human figure on the Finglesham buckle has only been found in the Baltic Sea area. Almost the exact same human figure was found in Thorslunda, in Öland, around AD 600 as a stencil for stamping bronze helmet plates. The human figure of Öland represents Odin, the Scandinavian name for Woden. This kind of representation of Woden was probably brought from Öland to Kent. Öland's archaeology deviates from the rest of Scandinavia's, because it has several stone castles from the Migration Era. Some of the castles had dwellings inside. Moreover, it seems as though these stone castles belonged to competing chieftain clans. It is clear from the find of many Roman coins that these clans participated in the wars with or against the Romans (perhaps with Attila's Huns or Saxons, who worshipped Woden?). When a Swedish chieftain came home to Öland, he may have brought the worship of Odin with him. It would have been natural for these Swedish chieftains to have contact with the Saxons in Kent as they had a similar religion.

Woden in figure 42 is characterised by two snakes fastened to his helmet. Corresponding representations of Odin in Scandinavia depict the two snakes as bird-headed. Likewise, the dancing warriors on the helmet from Sutton Hoo (figure 4) have two bird-headed snakes fastened to their helmets. Most probable is that the two bird-headed snakes are symbols of the Divine Twins, the creators of life. It is said, in a creation myth, that the first human being was created by Odin and his two brothers Vili ("will") and Ve ("yielding"). The two snakes are perhaps Vili and Ve. Woden dances on the Finglesham buckle (figure 42) holding two spears, just like he does in the Scandinavian representations of Odin. The spears and the dance refer to Odin as a warmonger.

Around AD 600, worship of Odin spread in Scandinavia, but worship of Woden simultaneously ceased in England due to the introduction of Christianity in Kent. The pagan King Ethelbert of Kent had married a Christian princess named Bertha, daughter of one of the Merovingian kings of the Franks. As a condition of her marriage, she had brought a bishop with her to Kent. In Ethelbert's capital of Canterbury, the bishop restored a church dating to Roman times, the current St Martin's Church. Bertha took the initiative to ask Pope Gregory the Great to send missionaries. Pope Gregory, the first monk, who became Pope, chose another monk in Rome, Augustine, to lead a mission to Britain in order to convert the pagan King Ethelbert of the kingdom of Kent to Christianity. Augustine arrived with 40 companions in AD 595.

The Aesir were predominantly worshipped in Kent by some of the chieftain class. In general, the Angles seem to retain the traditional religion as witnessed by the Sutton Hoo find (figures 4, 26, 27 and 59) and Franks Casket (figure 51). The first Christian missionary bishops successfully converted the Kentish royalty. Before the Saxon warrior groups arrived in England, they had lived for generations separated from their ethnic origin, sometimes as mercenaries, more often as pirates and raiders. The Saxons were, therefore, far more ready than the Angles to give up the old Germanic ways and adopt Christianity.

It is also vital to consider the difference between a cyclical religion and a saviour religion. In the old Germanic cyclical religion, there were oral rituals within the ethnic group and the individual could expect to be reincarnated within the community. Christianity and the Aesir religion are both saviour religions, whereby the faithful gain access to a community in heaven. This premise may have contributed to believers in the Aesir from the Kentish royalty converting to Christianity. Jesus Christ assumed Odin's place in Heaven. A second contributing factor for the successful conversion in some parts of England could be that the royals there were partly of British heritage and had preserved some of the Roman Christian culture.

In the chapter on the Angles in England, the process of strides between the tiny Germanic chiefdoms leading to the forming of slightly larger units is described. This process combined with increased inequality as the power became more centralised within the royal families. The Saxon kingdom of Kent was advanced and centralised. The first time we hear the title *Bretwalda*, ("ruler of Britain") it belongs to Ethelbert of Kent (ruled AD 560-616).

The mission in Kent was successful. Pope Gregory's missionaries described Jesus Christ as a mighty warrior, who could liberate the deceased from the world of death. The crucified Jesus was not depicted as suffering. Pope Gregory wrote to King Ethelbert that "Almighty God places good men in authority that He may impart through them the gifts of His mercy to their subjects". Thus, Ethelbert was promised God's blessing. After death, the blessed would be admitted into God's heaven. These ideas were not very different from the ideas of the Aesir religion. Ethelbert converted to Christianity and many followed him, because he was *Bretwalda*, the leading king of Britain. Augustine founded a monastery on land donated by the king, and was appointed the first Archbishop of Canterbury.

Augustine and Ethelbert also founded a school for Anglo-Saxons in Canterbury, where Christianity was taught in Latin as well as in old

English. This was the first school in a Germanic language in a Germanic country. Pope Gregory's missionaries used the language of the natives. Note their translation of the Latin names of the weekdays.

Latin	English	Saxon gods	Danish
dies lunae	Monday		Mandag
dies Martis	Tuesday	Tiw	Tirsdag
dies Mercurii	ednesday	Woden	Onsdag
dies Iovis	Thursday	Thunar	Torsdag
dies Veneris	Friday	Frija	Fredag
dies Saturni	Saturday		Lørdag
dies solis	Sunday		Søndag

The Catholic Church on the Continent had used the Latin names of the weekdays, which have their etymology in the Roman gods. Apparently four gods in the Aesir family correspond to the Roman gods. Obviously, it was not possible to find a Saxon god corresponding to the Roman god Saturn. When other Germanic speaking people, such as Old Saxons and Frisians, on the Continent were Christianised, they adopted similar names for the weekdays. The first Christianisation of Scandinavia took place around AD 1000 with the help of delegates from the Anglo-Saxon church. In Scandinavia, it was possible to find a word that resembled *Saturnus,* namely *Laukar,* meaning "healing" or "purification". Saturday was called *Laugar-dagr* later *Lørdag/ lördag* in the Scandinavian languages.

There are indications that the Saxons had these four gods before some of them immigrated to Britain – as suggested by Thunor and the hammer amulet discussed earlier (figure 41). Interestingly, both Woden and Frija are mentioned in a text written in Old High German. The *Merseburg Incantations,* the only known examples of Germanic pagan belief preserved in the language, are two magic spells. They were found in a theological manuscript written in the 9th or 10th century, although the charms themselves may be much older. Translated into English by D.L. Ashliman one of them says:

Phol and Wodan rode into the woods,
There Balder's foal sprained its foot.
It was charmed by Sinthgunt, her sister Sunna;
It was charmed by Frija, her sister Volla;
It was charmed by Wodan, as he well knew how:
Bone-sprain, like blood-sprain,
Like limb-sprain:
Bone to bone; blood to blood;
Limb to limb -- like they were glued.

The gods Wodan and Frija are mentioned; consequently, they must have been known by the pre-Christian Saxons on the Continent. The Sanskrit word *priya* means "dear, beloved, mistress, lady". The Germanic equivalent words are Freya, Frija, Frigga or Frea.

When the Saxon nobility converted to Christianity, the Aesir family of gods died out in England. However, many pagan traditions survived for centuries among the common people, in particular ideas relating to the old Vanir gods. When the Vikings raided England, they brought with them their Aesir religion once again. In the period AD 700-950, the great Scandinavian Viking kings believed in Odin and the Aesir. This was the religion of the rulers and a condition for their power. In this period, a lot of myths were created about the Aesir gods. Some were written down around AD 1200 and from these texts we know Nordic Mythology quite well. One of them, the poem *Völuspa* tells how the Aesir defeated the Vanir, forcing them to live in Heaven.

In this book, we will not deal with Odin and the Aesir anymore. The main subject is the old Germanic religion, but for now let's examine Anglo-Saxon warfare in more detail.

In the period AD 500-900, the Anglo-Saxon kings spent most of their time on warfare, trying to extend their power. All the people in England are now called Anglo-Saxons whether they are of Celtic, Anglo or Saxon origin.

According to *The Anglo-Saxon Chronicle,* Cerdic and his son Cynric came to England in AD 475 (reconciled time) with five ships and fought against the Welsh. Cerdic is a Celtic name and some authors doubt that he was Saxon (Myres 1986). It is more plausible that Cerdic was the head of a British noble family with extensive territorial interests in Hampshire. There is little material evidence for a Germanic presence in Hampshire in the AD 500s. The cemeteries have almost no cremations and the place names are predominantly Celtic.

AD 488 (reconciled time): Cerdic and Cynric slew a British king, named Natanleod, and five thousand men with him.

AD 499 (reconciled time): Cerdic and Cynric received the West-Saxon kingdom, and the same year they fought with the Britons, in the place now called Cerdicesford; the royal line of Wessex ruled from that day.

Around AD 502 (reconciled time): Cerdic battled at Mons Badonicus with the Britons from the upper Thames Valley and his defeat stopped his advance to the north.

The battle of Mount Badon stopped the Saxon conquerors for about 50 years. One of the proposals for the site of Badon is Badbury Rings, a fortification in Dorset near the Poole.

Archaeological finds in the Upper Thames Valley have shown that Angles and Britons lived there peacefully from the beginning of the

AD 400s. The Britons mostly lived in towns and the Angles lived in the countryside. Mixed cemeteries are a common occurrence here with inhumation burials of the Britons and cremation burials from the Germanic settlers. All settlers of the upper Thames arrived by boat up the Thames River.

The global climatic catastrophe in AD 540 and the plague, which reached the British Isles in AD 547 (the Plague of Justinian) gave rise to struggles over resources and new warlords seized power. Ceawlin and his people imposed their rule on the Britons and Angles in the Upper Thames Valley. In the *Anglo-Saxon Chronicle*, we read about his fights with neighbouring British warlords:

AD 560: Ceawlin obtained the West-Saxon kingdom.

AD 571: Battle of Bedcanford: here Cuthwulf fought against Britons at Bedcanford, taking the four settlements of Limbury, Aylesbury, Benson and Eynsham. He died that same year.

AD 577: Battle of Dyrham: here Cuthwine and Ceawlin fought against Britons, slaying three kings: Coinmail, Condidan and Farinmail, in the place which is called Dyrham as well as seizing the three towns of Gloucester, Cirencester and Bath.

AD 592: a great slaughter at Wodens Barrow. Ceawlin, who was called Saxon, lost to the Angles and Britons conspiring together.

These entries seem to show that the Britons' defences in the English Midlands collapsed. The Angles and Saxons united their areas and overran much of the plains of the Midlands. The loss of Bath to the Saxons separated the Welsh from the Britons of the south-west. After this, the border between Saxons and the south-west Celts was probably at the Wansdyke near Bath.

Ceawlin and his company called themselves *Gewisse*, meaning "reliable". They might have been a clan as their names begin with the letter C, but it is most likely that they were an alliance of warlords. They were not Saxons, but they established a kingdom that later was called West-Saxon. According to Kenneth Sisam's theory from 1953, the lineage of the West Saxon Monarchy was constructed in the AD 600s. At that time, the West Saxon kingdom was allied with the Bernician kingdom, the lineage of which was Woden—Baeldaeg—Brand. This was copied by the West Saxons, but instead of the Bernician ancestor, Benoc, the West Saxons introduced the Gewisse ancestor of Gewis. They also included Cerdic and Cynric from the first invasion. Later versions of the lineage of the royal house of Wessex included the names Freawine and Wig. Frowin and his son Wig were heroes in the old country, appearing in legends related to Istathe Syssel.

Each of the Anglo-Saxon kingdoms tried to increase their population and land. The king needed successful warfare to legitimate his position as king in relation to his subordinates as well as other nobles. A victory would hopefully result in rich looting and an extension of the kingdom. Warriors who proved their skill and brutality would be feared and receive precious gifts.

As early as the AD 500s, many small kingdoms absorbed each other. Norfolk and Suffolk united in AD 560. The old kingdom of Kent was squeezed and unable to expand. The kingdoms in Middle England could expand to the west at the expense of the Britons and became powerful: Northumbria in the AD 600s, Mercia in the AD 700s and Wessex in the AD 800s. Small kings who happened to live near them had to submit. Take for instance, Mercia, the last kingdom to accept Christianity.

Penda was a pagan warlord and later king of Mercia. He battled with other kings in Wessex and East Anglia but especially with the strong King Oswold of Northumbria. Penda was allied to the British (Welsh) king, Cynddylan. When Oswold visited the British area, Penda killed him and staked his body in what is now the town of Oswestry

("Oswold's tree"). Soon afterwards, Penda was attacked by the Northumbrian army lead by a bishop. A poem (*the Marwnad Cynddylan*) says that Cynddylan promised Penda "seven hundred men" for the battle, but that was probably the number of inhabitants in Cynddylan's kingdom. The battle took place at Lichfield ("corpse field") and many were killed including the bishop and Cynddylan.

The Staffordshire Hoard was discovered in a field near the village of Lichfield in 2009. Lichfield is located a few miles north of modern day Birmingham. The hoard, which consists of approximately 3,500 pieces, weighing at up to 5 kg of gold and 1.3 kg of silver, is the largest treasure of Anglo-Saxon gold and silver objects discovered to date. The contents include many finely worked silver and gold sword decorations that were removed from weaponry, including 86 sword pommels (Fig 42b). The only items in the hoard that were obviously not arms were two crosses. The warlike character suggests the hoard was not a deposit and the crosses being folded indicated the burial was a deposit was made by pagans. The hoard was deposited in a remote area, just south of a Roman road. There was no grave nearby so it could not have been a grave gift. Probably, it was a sacrifice made by a pagan king – Penda.

We do not know which gods Penda worshipped, but as sacrifices to Wodan were not given to the earth, it is most likely that the sacrifice

Fig 42b. Sword pommel from the Staffordshire Hoard near Lichfield in Mercia

was given to the Divine Twins. The decoration on the sword pommel in figure 42b probably shows the Divine Twins and is reminiscent of the buckle from Kent in figure 34 and the belt purse from Sutton Hoo in figure 27. Penda took the swords of slain enemies. The blades could be used again but the Germanics believed that gold belonged to the gods. Therefore, the sacrifice of the Staffordshire Hoard is comparable to the sacrifice of the golden horns in Gallehus. In both cases, the sacrifice was made before a great decision involving many people – decisions that needed help from the gods.

In AD 655, Penda invaded Bernicia (North Northumbria) with a large army. With Penda was the king of East Anglia, a British (Welsh) king and the king of Deira (southern Northumbria). Oswiu, king of Bernicia, tried to buy the invaders off. The British king accepted the bribe and went home. After which, the rest of the army withdraw. While retreating, Penda was attacked and there was a great battle. Penda's allies awaited the outcome from a place of safety. Penda lost the battle and his life at a place called Penda's Field near modern day Leeds.

Oswiu then had direct control of Mercia, but in AD 658, the nobles in Mercia revolted, throwing off Northumbrian rule. Penda's son, Wulfhere, then became king of Mercia. At that time, Mercia was surrounded by Christian kingdoms. It is uncertain whether or not Wulfhere was baptised, but he gave tracts of land to a few churches and allowed the visit of a bishop for the consecration. He also accepted a monastery in Peterborough, initially endowed by his Christian brother. Wulfhere became the most powerful king in southern Britain. In the AD 700s, Mercia had an even more powerful king: Offa. In his time, the kingdoms of Kent, East Anglia and Sussex disappeared. He led many raids in Wales and in order to secure the border he had "Offa's Dyke" built, one of England's greatest memorials to the past.

The Long Horn

The Angles in England followed the Germanic religion until being Christianised around AD 600, and many heathen ideas survived for centuries after. The golden horns are a unique source for studying the religion of the Angles as they belong to the same Anglian culture, thereby offering a careful description of human life.

The long horn, reconstructed in its entirety, had a plain horn inside made of gold alloy. The outside covering consisted of decorated rings made of pure gold. The upper seven rings were decorated with figures. Some of them were punched, and others were soldered figures. Interestingly, there were no stamps with pattern. The use of stamps with pattern came into being after AD 400, and are found in great number on the short horn, suggesting the earliest date for the short horn. Taken together, this indicates that the long horn is the oldest. Figure 43 shows the decoration of the upper seven rings, based on Ole Worm's original drawing. The rings are unfolded and the part on the concave side of the horn is pictured to the left.

Starting at the upper ring, due to its cryptic inscription, gives us the general meaning of the illustrations of the horn. There are two lines of figures: twelve figures in each line. Some of the figures are fairly similar to each other and they are repeated unsystematically, suggesting that the figures are cryptic letters. The assumption is that the text starts from the left in both lines – from the convex side of the horn. Moreover, the beginning of the text seems to be marked with a ball in the upper line and with a stick in the lower line. The two lines actually start with the same two-lettered word.

The language is old Germanic, and the only old Germanic we know is Gothic. Gothic is known from Wulfila's translation of the Bible into

Gothic in AD 340. The text was deciphered by the linguist Jens Juhl Jensen and the author (Rasmussen 1990):

EK IM UNMURDSA

EK ThIK GUIDA.

With the English translation: "I am the immortal, I guide you."

Before discussing the meaning of the text, it is necessary to examine the figures. On comparison, the figures in the two lines, which represent the same letter, are remarkably different. The lower figures are misfortunate; some of them are prisoners in chains and one has lost his hand, perhaps suggesting that the double snake between the lines is able to distinguish between good and bad and can guide man in the right direction.

It is rather clear that the long horn is an allegory of the individual human life. Ole Worm himself proposed this idea. The first six rings from the bottom depict different stages in life from conception to death (see figure 43).

Each of the six rings had a paragraph symbol that describes the stage. This symbol was placed on the concave side of the horn and is placed to the left in figure 43.

The conception is symbolised by two human bones, probably meaning the bones of some ancestor about to be reborn.

The foetus is symbolised by a plant with a bud. At birth, the flower will be seen.

The child is symbolised by two parents playing a board game. The little "devil" sits underneath the board, learning.

The worker is symbolised by a person carrying an axe and a digging stick, the most common tools for men and women.

The ruler is symbolised by a human wheel, meaning that that the ruler will fall and another ruler will assume power with his ruling sword.

The dead spirit is symbolised by the dead soul riding a horse and meeting a goddess in the land of the deceased who offers him the life elixir. This symbol is referred to as the "welcome symbol" in this book.

The friezes on the six rings are constructed in the same way: three symbols to the right of the paragraph symbol. In the middle is a symbol for the force of life or the will to live. On both sides of the force of life are symbols of the two guiding forces. The giving to the left and the receiving to the right. For instance, the stage of the child contains a fish, representing striving for life – the fish is endeavouring its way upwards to the next life stage. The guiding forces is two snakes with different attitude. However, not all the symbols will be examined in this book. The stage of the child will not be further examined.

The two-line inscription: *I am the immortal, I guide you* comes from the two snakes entwining each other between the two lines. The message is essential for understanding the decoration of the long horn: the invisible, punctured double snake guides man through the symbols and the various stages of life.

Inscription with ex-planation of the long horn

The dead soul

The ruler

The work-er

The child

The foetus

The con-ception

Fig 43. The decoration of the upper seven rings of the long horn, based on Ole Worm's drawing

The Double Snake

The double snake represents an immortal, invisible spirit. It is punctured in order to show its invisibility. The punctured, double snake features in many places on the long horn as it is watching man in different situations and guiding him through life. The snake is a common symbol in many cultures, symbolising primarily an underground force, but, in general, snakes can symbolise all kinds of invisible forces: spirits, natural forces or forces inside the human body, for instance, mental or physical diseases.

The double snake symbol was very popular with most of the Germanic tribes. Many so called snake-head-rings (such as that in figure 44) have been found in Germanic graves from Roman times (AD 1-400). Arm rings or finger rings of such type in gold or silver were used by members of the leading families within the tribe. .

Double snakes were also used as decoration on sword sheaths and shields. Figure 45 shows a piece of a sheath from AD 350 found in Nydam moor in Ellem Syssel. For the Germanic tribes, moors were

Fig 44. Gold arm ring from a rich grave in Nordrup, Zealand; around AD 250

Fig 45. Part of a sword sheath. Nydam Moor, Ellem Syssel, AD 350

places for sacrificing to the gods, and in the period AD 200-450, large quantities of weapons were dumped in moors, mainly in southern Jutland.

The Germanic tribes undoubtedly had names for the double snake. However, given we have only picture symbols of the Germanic gods and have no written documentation from the Germanics, the names of the gods are difficult to ascertain. Nevertheless, the Roman Tacitus in his work *Germania* from AD 100, briefly mentions the religion of the Germanics: "In their ancient songs, their only way of remembering or recording the past, they celebrate an earth-born god Tuisto, and his son Mannu, as the origin of their race, as their founders". *Tuisto* means "twisted", stemming from the word *two*, because a twist is normally comprised of two threads. It is probable that one name for the double snake was Tuisto. Tuisto came from the earth and could naturally appear in snake-form. It is notable that Tuisto existed before Mannus, the creator of human beings. Tuisto represents two universal qualities of life: giving and receiving. The Latin *Mannus* could be *Mannu* in the Germanic language. In old Indian Sanskrit literature, the creator of living creatures was *Manu*.

The double snake is not a uniquely Germanic symbol. In the Antique Middle East, bracelets and finger rings with two serpents or a serpent with a head on each end were popular, and they are found

148

Fig 46. Cadeceus. The staff of Hermes

in many places within the Mediterranean area. Take, for instance, the Caduceus staff. The two serpents entwining the staff represent the forces of giving and receiving, and the staff represents the equilibrium between these opposite forces. This staff belongs to the god Hermes, who is able to lead and find the right way, and the wings denote his ability to fly. Sometimes the wings adorn his hat. The Cadeceus is also the symbol utilised by physicians and pharmacists, those who try to heal.

Another well-known example of the double snake is the Yin Yang symbol from Chinese Taoism (figure 47). Although the symbol is now very stylised, its early form in China was two serpents or two dragons entwined. *Yin* is the receiving or ingoing force and *Yang* is the giving or outgoing force, contraction and expansion, enjoying and helping, passive and active.

The idea of a pair of snake-gods was also widespread among the pre -Columbian Americans. Two rings, such as that in figure 48, were found in the Mayan town of Chicken-Itza in Mexico. They were

Fig 47. Yin Yang symbol

placed at either ends of a playing ground. The losing team was the one whose ring the ball passed through. Some of the losers were then sacrificed. Most likely, the ring is a symbol for being birthed to a new life and the ball, a symbol for the soul. The two snakes are guiding the process of rebirth. The Aztecs, who ruled over the majority of the Mayan people, also worshipped two snake gods, who were born from the bosom of Mother Earth. One of them, Quetzalcoatl, ("the feathered twin") was the god of the sky at daytime. The other one, Tezcatlipoca, was god of the sky at night.

The idea of two forces controlling life is widespread in general. These forces could be conceived as gods, but not as ordinary gods. They go together. They can take any form in the outside world. They are also found inside man. This pair of gods has had many names and forms and are sometimes called the Divine Twins. This religion is natural in the sense that it describes the nature of the world inside and outside. The sun goes up and down. The moon waxes and wanes. The earth gives life to plants and animals and also takes care of the dead. Essentially, all creatures produce and consume. It is the way in which nature works – with the help of the two forces. When we exploit the earth, we have to give something back. The relation

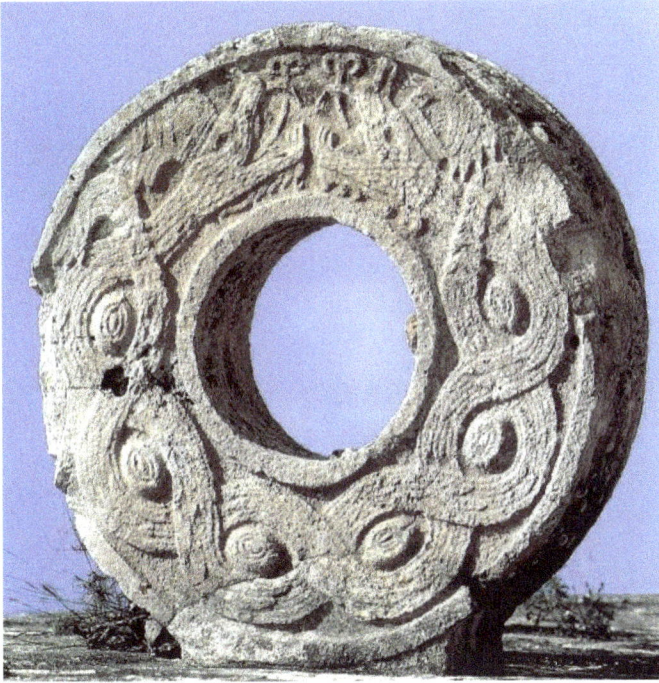

Fig 48. Stone ring used for religious ball playing by Mayans at Chicken-Itza, Mexico, AD 900

to other people must be helpful and joyful. These ideas are not propagated in modern society, but perhaps they are manifesting themselves again in organic and sustainable production.

The two forces control the exterior world as well as the interior one. They are present in the human body and mind. One state of mind is activity, resolution and talking, corresponding to the giving force (Yang). The other state of mind is attention, perceiving and listening, corresponding to the receiving force (Yin). Modern brain research has shown that the giving state normally involves activity in the left hemisphere of the brain, while the receiving state involves activity in the right hemisphere. This fundamental characteristic of the human brain may be one reason that the idea of the Divine Twins was so popular and omnipresent in Antiquity. Both forces are essential for life.

In modern society, the receiving force in the mind has been underestimated. Observing and attention have little prestige. However, the popularity of "mindfulness" highlights some interest in these matters. Perhaps we could learn something from the old wisdom?

The Worker

We start with the stage of the worker in the fourth ring from the bottom in figure 43. To the left, the concave side of the horn, we have the general symbol for the stage, a person who carries an axe and a pick – the most common tools for men and women. To the right, in every stage, there are three soldered figures explaining how the three fundamental forces in life influence the actions of humanity. In the middle, we have courage, or the will to live, surrounded by the two steering forces: the giving to the left and the receiving to the right. Courage is symbolised in the worker stage by an advancing and roaring calf. This animal grows fast, representing "fattening" or meat production. The sheep-dog, to the left, is a symbol of indefatigable work. The active dog is jumping up high with open eyes and ears. The lazy dog, to the right, is lying down, sleeping with closed eyes and ears, representing carefree enjoyment.

But what of the punctured snake figures in the worker stage? Both punctures and snakes represent invisible forces; spiritual forces in the mind. The twisted, double snake is placed under the active dog in order to emphasise the importance of active work. The giving snake has a bird's tail. It starts to fly up to the active dog, but comes to its senses and unites in a twist with the receiving snake. The receiving snake has a forked fishtail. After a twist, it closes its eyes and falls asleep. The calf has a simple mind, suggested by the two punctuated lines through its body. But the calf seems to be aware of the punctuated flower cross. This symbol appears six times in the uppermost ring and could be a symbol of heavenly beauty and wisdom. The cross was a traditional symbol of the spiritual world long before Christianity. The punctuated snake, behind the active dog, illustrates a mind turning round, ruminating, and probably "going around the bend". Sheep-dogs work themselves to death.

Finally, we see the lazy dog's mind as a fat, punctuated snake with a fish tail lying on its back with closed eyes. But this dreaming or contemplating act makes it possible for the soul to fly as illustrated with the punctuated snake above the lazy dog.

The artist has described the worker's life without uttering a single word. The choice of picture symbols is unique and we should not expect to find similar examples from other artists. Therefore, interpreting it is a matter of judgement. The meaning seems to be that the worker should be aware of the beauty and wisdom in the spiritual world. If he has confidence in his kinsmen and in the spiritual powers, he will be happy. He should be active and work hard most of the time, but he should not lose his head and work himself to the bone. He should rest and clear his mind in order to find purpose of his activity. A moral typical of Germanic religion. Nothing is absolutely good or bad. It depends on the circumstances.

The long horn describes those stages of human life where farming and cattle breeding was essential. The advice for the individual is to work hard, but to keep in mind the heavenly wisdom of the spiritual world. There are no laws in Germanic religion. It belongs to the tribe. Thus, you have to work for the common good and you will be protected by your fellow tribe members.

The Ruler

The stage of the ruler comes next in figure 43. The general symbol of the ruler is a wheel made of two naked persons growing together. Undoubtedly, deities – probably the Divine Twins, who, according to some myths, always stick together. The wheel represents the daily turn of Heaven as well as the circle of life and both are driven by the Divine Twins. A number of decoration plates, such as that in figure 49, have been found near Wiesbaden, in Germany, and despite dating to the AD 600s, the symbolism is obviously the same as the symbol at the stage of the ruler.

The ruler in the human community could be the older leading person in the family or the leader of the tribe. As usual, three soldered figures that show how the three forces of life influence the action of man are present, signifying three different attitudes available to the leader – three kinds of power. The lion-man, to the left, represents

Fig 49. Decoration plate of bronze from Niederursel, near Wiesbaden, Germany, AD 600s

physical power and strength. Perhaps a hero. The lion-man holds his arms the same way shamans or worriers do when they dance in a trance, so the lion-man also represents agitation and boldness. He is the giving force. The man, to the right, denotes economic power, justice and the law. The axe is the symbol of the farmer, the landowner. His bird mask tells us that he may voice his rights, but he has no ears and does not listen. The landowner receives the surplus of the workers' production. He is the receiving force. In the middle is spiritual power. This man has a sword, a symbol of a leader and a decision maker. He has a wolf's mask with ears, indicating that he listens. The two figures with masks open their mouths and talk to each other. The leader has a dispute with the landowner. The leader has the will to find a way, the will to go on.

Punctured snakes are present on this ring, too. The twisted double snake sits under the landowner, emphasising that consideration of economy and rights of property are essential for ruling. The lion-man's body is filled with a punctuated snake meaning that his body and soul are one and the same. He is pointing up towards a snake, which may point to his agitated soul leaving his body. He is willing to give his life for the community. The landowner has a punctuated snake that twists first to the right and then to the left. It seems that – on this horn – a twist to the left suggests moving forward and twist to the right means moving backward. Thus, the mind of the landowner is moving back and forth, implying that he is hesitating, unable to make a decision. The snakes at the spiritual leader always twist to the left, encircling him and he himself is turning. He must be aware of the physical power of the lion-man, but has no dialogue with him. He is more aware of the economic power of the axe-man and his snake teaches him with his index finger.

The meaning of the decoration of this ring seems to be this: the ruler should consider both the giving and receiving forces. The enthusiastic or agitated attitude of the lion-man needs to be employed from time to time. However, most important for the ruler is to think clearly and listen to the landowner, who represents material reality. Thereby, the ruler obtains a realistic view of the situation, which he can decipher and then make a decision on to the benefit the family and/or the tribe. The ruler is in a different situation to the worker. Normally, the ruler is old and the worker is young. The double snake emphasises the ruler's receiving force and the workers' giving force. In Germanic thinking, there is no good or bad behaviour. What is best depends on the situation. There is no moral sin or virtue in the modern sense.

This insight is very relevant to understanding Germanic tribal society. Here, all tribe members were farmers as well as warriors. There was no king and his army to protect the tribe. In the case of war, all men had to fight.

The Welcome Symbol

The next ring depicts the dead soul as seen in figure 43. The general illustration shows the dead soul riding on a flying horse to the realm of the deceased, where it is offered a welcome drink from a goddess, representing the assured continued life of the dead spirit. This scenery, referred to here as "the welcome symbol", was used by Germanic tribes, but it first appeared in Scandinavia after the end of the Migration Age in AD 575, confirming that the long horn was produced in Roman times somewhere south of Scandinavia. The welcome symbol is quite common among the earlier Sarmatian tribes in the Ukraine (see figure 28), and it was first used by some southern Germanic tribes (Goths and Saxons) who were influenced by Sarmatian riding culture.

Around AD 700, the welcome symbol appears simultaneously on many gravestones in Gotland and on a few amulets found in

Fig 50. Guldgubbe from Helgö, Sweden and from Lundeborg, Funen, Denmark

Denmark. Another version of the welcome symbol is seen on the small gold foil figures called *guldgubber* in Danish. Thousands of them have been found in Scandinavia, dating from AD 575-700, mostly near posts of contemporary domestic houses, probably representing the goddess Freya and played perhaps a role in her worship. They are the size of a fingernail and so thin that they could only be fastened with glue to a post in the house.

Figure 50 shows two examples. On guldgubber the deceased is not riding a horse, but often has a pick instead – the principle being the same as on the welcome symbol. The *guldgubbe* in figure 50b depicts a drinking horn, while on the other one, the goddess has an enormous square-headed brooch at her neck. In Norse mythology, the goddess Freya or one of her helpers, the Valkyries, welcomed the souls of deceased warriors. They could fly like birds and fetch the spirit of the dead. Freya also had a cloak of feathers as seen in figure 50a. Freya also had a marvellous piece of jewellery called *Brísingamen* ("brilliant piece of jewellery"). In *Beowulf* line 1197, it says the "Brosinga Men" belonged to a southern Germanic King. Worm's drawing (figure 43) features a bearded, long-haired man with the drinking horn instead of the goddess who is seen on all other welcome symbols. Ole Worm probably mistook the brooch for a beard.

The original name of the goddess Austra, Eostra was probably the only one used in southern Scandinavia until the migration of the Angles, because they brought only this name to England. Traditional Scandinavian girls' names such as *Estrid* and *Astrid* bear witness to the goddess' name *Eostur*. On the other hand, as mentioned in the chapter entitled "The two Warriors", Vinniler worshipped "Frea" when they arrived in what is now northern Germany in the AD 100s. The legend was written down in the AD 600s. Perhaps a name similar to *Frea* was first used in northern Germany. Likewise, the Saxons used, and brought with them to England, the word *Frija* from where the

Fig 51. Franks Casket, the right side

word Friday stemmed in the AD 600s. The names Freya, Frija, Frea and Frig used to denote the goddess by the different Germanic people are all related to the Indo-European *priya* meaning "dear, beloved, mistress".

Another example of the welcome symbol worth noting is Franks Casket; a casket of whale bone carved on all four sides and the top with illustrations and explanations in runes. It was probably made in Northumbria in the AD 680s. Most of the illustrations illustrate the Divine Twins' influence on the life of a warrior. Figure 51 shows the right side of the casket with a description of the warrior's death. The explanation for the illustration is a poem written in old Germanic runes. Below is my translation (Rasmussen 2005):

The High Goddess sits on the harm full hill
The swift one (the horse) draws so as her Earth Mother did prescribe
Wounding, the caretaker and the saviour will remove.

The illustration in figure 51 is like a cartoon. The first line of the text describes the scene to the left: the warrior meeting his death on the hill, where a goddess sits clad in feathers, implying she is the goddess who bestows and takes life. The goddess Eostra had

160

approximately the same function for the Angles as the goddess Freya had in Norse mythology. It is noteworthy that Eostra has the head of a hare as it was a symbol of reproduction due to its procreative powers. Eostra was worshipped in the Easter month (April) and her hare symbol played a role in the spring rituals. In south-eastern England there is evidence of a custom of hare-hunting on Good Friday. The heathen Easter Bunny/Hare/Rabbit is popular worldwide today.

Thereafter, comes a flying horse and above it is written "RISKI" meaning "quick". We see the Earth Mother receiving the warrior, whose body has already been interred in the grave below. In front of the Earth Mother is a drinking cup with the inscription "BITE" meaning "drink". Finally, the Divine Twins are called "the caretaker" and "the saviour", supporting the dead soul on his journey through the realm of the dead.

A similar situation adorns the Sutton Hoo purse (figure 27): a man with a death mask and his arms locked and supported by two wolves. The symbols featured on Frank's Casket and the Sutton Hoo purse are contemporary in time and culture, denoting the dead soul being guided through the realm of death by the Divine Twins. It is no surprise that the Divine Twins take the form of wolves. The two dogs of the underworld was an old Germanic idea as is evident on the Gold Horn (figure 57) and on a grave gift (figure 61). Dogs in the underworld are also known in Greek Mythology.

The Dead Soul

To return to the long horn and the ring of the dead soul. This ring is peculiar because the welcome symbol is not just a segment but rather an essential part of the life of the dead soul. The welcome drink from the goddess ensures that the dead soul will live on. Therefore, all the soldered figures on this ring, including the welcome symbol, are accompanied by a punctured figure (symbolising the inner life of the person).

As always, and as is characteristic of this horn, three soldered figures representing the three forces of life are present. The giving force, to the left, is represented by a walking man pointing at his legs. He is raised because he is a ghost walking in the air. He continues walking and probably has tired legs, thus the arrows pointing at his legs may indicate pain. He is clinging to his past life among the living. Ghosts that cannot find rest are not popular among living people. The active giving force is not recommended in this stage of life.

The deer hunt is a very old and widespread symbol for the travelling dead soul. It is found on rock carvings, seal stones and pottery. An example of this is seen in figure 61. The deer represents the new life. It is also a symbol of the sun moving below the Earth. The sun is reborn every morning. The archer with the pointing arrow denotes the attentiveness of the soul following the deer/ the sun. He does not kill the deer but when the deer is reborn he might also be. The archer in this ring represents the will to live, He has his concentration to the right side, where we find the receiving force represented by the deer running away. When the soul wants to be reborn it must give up and forget everything from the past life and be like an animal without memories, as demonstrated by the deer.

Draw your attention to the double snake beside the deer. Here, we see the two snakes with human upper parts and the human beings resemble babies. They clap their hands happy to be meeting each other and happy to be attending the conception of a new human life. In fact, they assist themselves by taking place inside the coming parents, guiding the parents to sexual intercourse and sharing in the delight. They also make some special loops with their tails, which perhaps represent the mating of the two sexes as loops are symbols of energy. Similar loops are seen at the ring of conception performed by a pair of dolphins.

From the long horn, we know that the two guiding forces of the double snake can help in all stages of life. They even assist with the conception and birth of a new human being as depicted in several examples of Germanic art. A gravestone from Gotland (figure 52) shows Mother Earth sitting in a birthing position, assisted by two snakes. It is worth noticing that one snake, the giving force, has the beak of a bird of prey whereas the other one has the beak of a web-footed bird. The decoration on the gravestone clearly expresses hope for the rebirth of the buried person.

For the Angles and most heathen Germanics, the soul existed before conception. The invisible soul could have a long history, taking up

Fig 52. Carving at a gravestone from Gotland, around AD 500

Fig 53. The "Spongman". Lid of an urn found at the Spong Hill cemetery

abode in different creatures. It could even be the soul of a deceased human. For example the Danish hero Halga is said to have been reborn. Different ethnic groups could have had different ideas regarding how the dead soul travelled, and different delineations of the life of the soul are found.

One of the many urns at the Spong Hill cemetery, in North-Elmham, had an unusual figure on the lid. Archaeologists cannot agree on the meaning of the so-called "Spongman" (figure 53). Indeed, it is difficult to identify it as either male or female. However, a skirt and the lack of a beard point to female. The seated position, with the elbows on the knees, is not godlike but rather indicates resting and waiting dead soul. The arms are made unnaturally long so that the hands could be held behind the ears. The eyes are wide open. The figure is listening and watching. And what would a dead soul be aware of if not the goddess of regeneration? The goddess of regeneration, according to the Angles, was Eostra. But as the figure is so exceptional the god of resurrection may even be the Christian God.

The Origin of the Long Horn

Let us return to the encrypted text on the uppermost ring. The human figures have very strange postures. Probably in an attempt to depict letters, which have been deciphered previously (for more see Rasmussen 1990):

EK IM UNMURDSA

EK ThIK GUIDA.

The reader may verify from the encrypted inscription on the long horn (figure 43) and the alphabets (figure 54), that the encrypted letters resemble Venetic letter symbols and not runic letter symbols.

Of the several alphabets found in the Alpine areas, the Venetic is one of the best known. These north Alpine alphabets were related to Etruscan. They disappeared around AD 50 when Latin letters became universal.

An inscribed cross-bow style fibula was found in a woman's grave in Meldorf, in West Holstein, dating to AD 40 (figure 55). These old inscriptions had no standard direction, but this one is read right to left. The inscription is transcribed as "IRILI", meaning "made by the eril". Many runic inscriptions, with old Germanic runes, were made by an eril, who was, as we have seen, the chieftain and religious leader

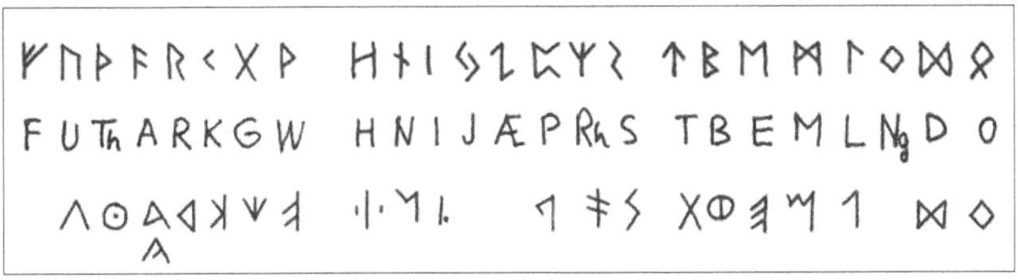

Fig 54. The runic alphabet with pronunciation (second row) and the corresponding Venetic letters (third row)

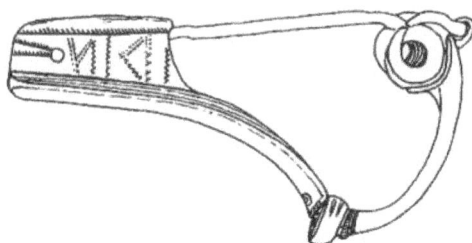

Fig 55. Fibula from Meldorf, West Holstein, AD 40

of the tribe (*eril* being "spokesman" from "oral", and later becoming *jarl* in Scandinavia and *earl* in Britian). The eril could apply to both foreigners and gods. Many Germanic tribes called their leader *eril*; thus, the Romans called these tribes *Heruli*.

If the figures on the long horn correspond to north Alpine letters, then this is an indication that the long horn is much older than the short horn, probably produced before AD 50. Furthermore, some of the symbols on the long horn were not used in Scandinavia in the AD 400s. For example, the wheel of two gods from the ring of the leader (figure 43) was not used in Scandinavia, but, according to the bronze plate in figure 49, it was well known on the right side of the Rhine near Wiesbaden.

Another foreign symbol on the horn is the two playful dolphins on the ring of conception (figure 43), a symbol of mating dance and conception. The playful dolphins have a more profound meaning, representing the Divine Twins, who ensure the creation of new life. The Dolphin symbol is Mediterranean in origin. The symbol has been found on gravestones in several places throughout the Roman Empire. Figure 56 shows the gravestone of a Roman officer in Wiesbaden. The inscription says he came from the contemporary Italian town of Brescia.

Fig 56. Gravestone from Wiesbaden

Rome had their strongest army of eight Roman legions stationed on the west bank of the Rhine, near Cologne and Wiesbaden. This area grew rich and jewellery and precious weapons were produced here. Allied Germanic ethnic groups called *Auxilia*, who fought under their own command, were also stationed here. The Germanics acquired gold through warfare so the gold for the long horn may have been earned from serving the Romans.

In AD 9, three Roman legions were eliminated in an ambush at Teuteburg, east of the Rhine by an alliance of Germanic tribes including some Chaucis. The Germanics were lead by Hermann (Latin: *Armenius*). In AD 15, a Roman army of 60,000 men, lead by Germanicus, sought revenge by initiating campaigns of destruction east of the Rhine. The Roman army burned villages, killed and took slaves. The Germanics fled into the woods. When Germanicus and some of the army retreated by boat from the Weser River, they sailed into a storm in the North Sea and were shipwrecked. Germanicus survived and was saved by the Chauci in their land. The Chauci then allied themselves with Germanicus. It came to a head the following year in a great battle at the Weser River between the Germanics and the Romans. Many Germanics fell and Hermann was wounded. He smeared his face with his own blood to disguise his identity, urged his horse onward towards the Roman left wing, which was occupied by the Chauci. Some have said he was recognised by Chauci serving among the Roman auxiliaries, who let him go. The Romans were victorious in many battles with Hermann, but the war was too expensive, so they subsequently ceased warfare east of the Rhine.

When an ethnic group of Germanics partook in war, they brought with them a chieftain, an *eril*. It is very likely that the eril of the Chauci who joined Germanicus was rewarded with gold and had the long horn made. The long horn describes an individual human and his inner life, and does not relate to the gods of any tribe. It is probable that it was produced for an eril of the Chauci by a goldsmith in the area near Wiesbaden. Soldiers from all parts of the Empire met here and many of them received gold from plunder or in salary. This was probably also the best place for a goldsmith to be.

If the long horn was produced near Wiesbaden, another question is also answered. The welcome symbol on the ring of the dead soul (figure 43) was not been found in Scandinavia until the AD 600s. Therefore, the long horn was produced by a goldsmith who had contact with the Sarmatian culture. This would be possible in the area near Wiesbaden because some of the *auxilia* were Iazygian (Sarmatian).

Following this theory, we have to ask the subsequent questions: how was the long horn transported to southern Jutland? And how was the horn preserved for 400 years? The answers can only be speculations. The transportation was carried out by the eril, when he returned from war service. There are several examples of Germanic warriors returning from military service with precious Roman artefacts. In the period AD 1-200, the so-called Over-Jersdal culture was common to southern Jutland, Holstein and Haduloha. The name Chauci ("the Hackers" – probably due to the hatchets they fought with) was used by the Romans and the Chauci may have been an association of ethnic groups. One of these groups may then have been based in southern Jutland. The inscription on the Meldorf fibula was made by another eril in Holstein, possibly Chauci.

In the AD 000s, we have the first ring fortress in Scandinavia. Trælbanke in Ellem Syssel near Gallehus (see figure 7) has a ring wall with a height of 1.5 m and diameter of 90 m. Outside the wall is a moat 1 m deep. Carbon[14] dating and potsherds both indicate that the fortification was used at the time. A contemporary village was found near Kærgård, 500 m from Trælbanke with at least 3 houses. They were long houses with three functions: habitation, barn and stable. This type was found in northern Germany and Istathe Syssel. On the island of Sylt, near Gallehus, two ring walls from the same period can be seen: Achsumburg, with a diameter of 70 m, and Tinnumburg, with a diameter of 120 m and a height of 7 m. There was once a third ring wall on Sylt, Rantumburg, but it is now covered by dunes.

These fortifications were probably constructed by people who had participated in wars and now wanted to establish a safe, military position. The name of the group is unknown, but they were possibly part of the Chauci association. Ptolemy's Map of the islands along the west coast of Jutland names them Alokiai Nesoi. In Ellem Syssel, we find a tribe called *Chali*, which may refer to the *Alikones* ("the prosperous tribe").

The preservation of the long horn for hundreds of years indicates that the Chauci tribes were self-confident in their culture and maintained their traditions for a very long time, as supported by the evidence. Tacitus, writing in AD 98, described the inland, non-coastal Chauci homeland as immense, densely populated and well-stocked with horses. He was effusive in his praise of their character as a people, saying that they were the noblest of the Germans, preferring justice to violence, being neither aggressive nor predatory, but militarily capable and always prepared for war should the need arise.

The Short Horn

Unfortunately, the short horn was missing its bottom and only the five uppermost rings were preserved. Three independent drawings of the short horn exist. The best one, by Paulli, is shown in figure 57. On comparison, the four rings of the long horn, referred to here as:

The dead soul

The ruler

The worker

The child

resemble the same stages of life as the corresponding four rings of the short horn. For example, it is obvious that the human wheel and the lion-man represent the ruler's ring on both horns. As the horns were found in the same place, the creator of the short horn must have been familiar with the long horn, and his layout was probably inspired by the much older long horn. But the attitude is quite different on the two horns: the long horn focuses on the behaviour of the individual and the inner life, and uses three symbols to describe a stage of human life: the giving force, the force of dedication and the receiving force. The double-snake gives the individual some advice for how to handle these forces.

The short horn does not say anything about these inner forces. Rather, the short horn describes the outside world as perceived by members of the tribal society. Forces in the outside world include natural forces and spiritual forces, such as deities and ancestral spirits. The short horn gives us a Germanic picture of the universe including divine powers. The predominant three powers are the same as those seen on the long horn: the will to live and the two guides that are the giving and receiving forces. They take different forms on the short horn.

Four out of the seven picture rings of the long horn are addressed here, and three of the five rings of the short horn are examined.

Fig 57. The five rings of the short horn as recorded by Paulli

Tiw

Beginning with the uppermost ring of the short horn (figure 2), which represents Heaven, the most prominent figure is the horned animal. This stag or bull symbolises the Germanic heavenly god Tiw, whose name means bull or steer. The bull Tiw was worshipped by many Germanic tribes and even by some tribes of the Migration Age. Several bull idols by Germanic tribes have been found. Figure 58 shows a bronze bull found alongside other cult figures in the religious centre of Gudme on Funen.

Tiw resided in heaven like the Greek god Zeus, who similarly was a bull. The names *Tiw*, *Zeus* and the Latin name for god, *Deus,* all have the same Indo-European origin. The Old High German name *Tiwaz*. One of the Germanic runes has the name *Tir* meaning "bull" (figure 75). In Nordic Mythology, the name of the god was *Tyr,* meaning "bull". Later, we will see that the Germanic god Tiw was known as the creator of the world in some myths. In some tribes, the bull Tiw/Tyr was a stag, which was one of the animals represented in Scandinavian rock carvings from the Bronze Age. The golden horns

Fig 58. Bronze bull with horns and silver eyes from Gudme on Funen, AD 300s

belonged to a tribe in southern Jutland that worshipped the heavenly stag as evident in the depictions on the short horn (figure 2). Celtic and Slavic tribes also adored the divine stag, but used other monikers.

Evidence for the worship of the stag can be found in *Beowulf* – unfortunately, no names of the heathen god exist:

Of halls the noblest: Heorot he named it
Whose message had might in many a land.
Not reckless of promise, the rings he dealt,   80
Treasure at banquet: there towered the hall,
High, gabled wide, the hot surge waiting.

The name of the hall "Heorot" in line 78 means "Hart". Note that in line 82 the hall was said to be adorned with horns.

Divine bulls and stags or any other animal gods were not the biological kind. They were invincible forces with qualities similar to the animals in question. The bull has always been the emblem of pro -creative power. The biological bull takes care of the herd, keeping the herd together; it reproduces and defends against outsiders. The bull is a symbol of solidarity within a community, a totem for the group. We see such symbols of solidarity among clans, tribes, nations, lodges, football supporters and so on, quite often animal symbols. Like a bull, Tiw protected the tribe and the "Thing", where all free men from the tribe could meet and make decisions, even if that was going to war. Consequently, Tiw became a god of war.

Tiw was a god of the Saxons before the Wotan had even been heard of. Similarly, Tyr was a Scandinavian god before Odin arrived. Tiw was accepted among the Aesir ("high"), because he resided in heaven. However, the Aesir were worshipped by the ruling class, who trusted Odin would ensure their victory. The rulers did not have close relations to the people and only common people made battle sacrifices to Tyr. In fact, only one myth concerns Tyr within Nordic Mythology. The wolf, Fenrir, who represented violent death to human beings, grew up among the Aesir. Fenrir became so huge and fierce that only Tyr was willing to feed him. In order to lay the wolf in chains, it was necessary for one of the gods to put his hand in between the wolf's great jaws. Only Tyr was willing to do this – losing his hand in the process. Tyr was ready to sacrifice himself for the community and, thus, represents courage and solidarity.

Angles from southern Jutland worshipped the divine stag and presumably brought this tradition with them to England, as is evident from pottery decorated with deer in southern Jutland and in England. The stag of the Gold Horn (figure 2) is another indication. An outstanding example is a stone sceptre from the Sutton Hoo ship burial. The sceptre is a royal treasure of King Redwald of East Anglia (figure 59). The sceptre consists of a long whetstone and figure 59 shows only its upper half. The whetstone was symbolic in meaning because the king was to approve the application of weapons and sharpen them. The young stag symbolises the Anglian king's solidarity with the people of East Anglia. This kind of solidarity would probably not be found among so-called Saxon kings. They belonged to different ethnic group than the people they ruled over and had more solidarity with their own family.

The stag on the sceptre is placed on top of a ring, which was a common symbol for heaven. For that reason, we here see the heavenly stag. Eight faces are carved on the whetstone in oval frames: four above and four below. Each face has individual features. Three have beards. Depictions of similar contemporary faces have been found in Scandinavia. It is safe to assume these faces represent deceased ancestors.

Fig 59. Top of the whetstone sceptre from the Sutton Hoo ship burial

It is possible that the Red Horse of Tysoe, near Warwick in Mercia, had something to do with Tiw (figure 60). It is reconstructed from a series of photographs by Graham Miller and Kenneth Carrdus. The name *Tysoe* has been suggested as meaning "Tiw's hoh", meaning a spur of land dedicated to the god Tiw. However, the Red Horse of Tysoe resembles more a bull than a horse. We do not know when the contour was cut into the red clay ground for the first time. Anglian tribes were fighting for land in Mercia in the AD 500s, so it is possible that they worshipped the tribal god Tiw by cutting his picture into the ground in Tysoe. Place names related to Tiw can be found at several places in England. In Oxfordshire, for instance, we have Great Tew and Dus Tew.

Fig 60. Outline of the Red Horse of Tysoe, 76 x 61m

The idea of the heavenly bull as a symbol for the people survived in southern Jutland much longer than in England. As testified by the sceattas minted in Ribe around AD 710. At that time, the Christian monk Willibrord visited the heathen king Angentheow in southern Jutland. If we look at the so called "Monster" on the back side of the sceattas (figure 25) we see the heavenly bull flying in heaven. The bull turns around and comes back just like heavenly daylight comes back. The sun symbol indicates that it is daytime. The pattern on the body and the horns shows the procreative power of the bull. The three dots and the bow with three loops are symbols of the three forces of life.

Deer and Dogs

The second ring from the top of the short horn (figure 57) represents the dead soul and the underworld. On the concave side, (that is to the left in figure 57) we find the deer hunt symbol. As with the long horn, this symbolises the journey of the dead soul. The dear represents the sun and when the dead soul follows the sun under the Earth he might be reborn like the sun. However, there are a few differences. The archer now wears a peasant's coat. On this horn humans wear clothes. Gods are naked because they do not require clothes. The arrow of the bow is very heavy like a pointer signifying the dead soul following the arrow to the deer, and then the deer into a new life.

The deer has a double contour probably indicating it was only a contour soldered onto the horn. The same technique is used for the deer on the uppermost ring. Perhaps implying the deer is a vision. The deer is not material. The two deer are symbols for the sun. The

Fig 61. Deer hunt. Stone carving from Bjergagergård, southern Jutland, 600 BC

deer with horns on the uppermost ring represents the sun above the Earth's surface, the upper world. The strange horns probably lift up the sun across heaven. The symbol of a heavenly stag dragging the sun is a well-known symbol even from the Bronze Age. The deer of the underworld represents the force that moves the sun in the night below the Earth's surface. It has large ears for listening in the dark night. The deer and the sun pass through the underworld in a night, but the archer is not expected to go so fast as long as he keeps to his course.

The animal under the deer on the underworld ring of the short horn has been taken as a sucking fawn but the two other drawings of the short horn show that it has to be a dog hunting the deer. There is another dog on this ring placed across a moon sickle. Thus, the dog represents the moon's force. The two dogs probably represent the waxing and waning of the moon. On the uppermost ring, we see two wolves or dogs on either side of the deer. They also represent the moon's phases. In the real sky, the waxing moon is to the left of the sun. Consequently, the left dog in the upper world represents the waxing moon. The tail of the dog imitates the form of the waxing moon.

Beside the left dog of the waxing moon, on the ring of heaven in figure 57, is found two special stamps, which resemble arrows. The two stamps are also found on the ring of dead souls beside the moon dog, and they with the dog of the waxing moon on the ring of the worker. The special stamps could be date marks. The Germanic people and all non-writing people kept track of dates with the help of the full moon and the new moon.

A careful look at the ring in two stamps, beside the dog of the waxing moon, reveals that the lower one is empty but the upper one contains two minor rings, probably suggesting they symbolise the new moon and the full moon, respectively. The real waxing moon is seen between the new moon and the full moon.

The moon and the moon dogs are depictions of the giving and receiving forces. The giving force, here the waxing moon, is seen to the left and the receiving force to the right like on the long horn.

Figure 61 is an example of the deer hunt symbol, which is found in graves of many societies. This one, dating to 600 BC, was found in a bog with sacrifices in southern Jutland. The hunter has a spear. We see two dogs and a stag with antlers. The hunter represents the dead soul. Again, the deer represents the sun and the dogs represent the moon phases. The dead soul must follow these celestial bodies into the underworld in order to be reborn.

It is difficult for modern man to understand the use of animal symbols. Indeed, it is not biological animals that should come to mind. These animals are fantastic monsters representing cosmic powers, and the particular animal is chosen, because of its characteristic powers. The sun and daylight have those specific qualities of the deer: stately, full of vitality during the day, invisible but alert at night, fast moving, harmless and productive. The real moon moves to and from the sun like dogs hunting a deer. Therefore, the hunting dogs have the same qualities as the moon. Religious ideas are myths; spoken imaginings. Like any other story or explanation, they belong to the spiritual world and not to the material world. Pictures and figures are also stories and belong to the spiritual life. Pictures quite often depict ideas and myths that are invisible in the physical world. Artists of antiquity were conscious of expressing ideas and myths that were essential in life. Thus, naturalistic images were inadequate.

Serpents

In the lower world, on the short horn (figure 57), we also see a long serpent, which has a little ball in its mouth that it is bringing up to the upper world. The snake lives in the earth and is appropriate for carrying something through the underworld. This serpent is obviously an invisible spiritual force. Two smaller serpents can also be seen. Their accompanying dots signifying their spiritual nature. They probably represent the giving force and the receiving force; the two universal forces here – the divine twins guiding the large serpent through the lower world.

Serpents are found in other contexts related to the dead, such as the Bronze Age carving in figure 61. Another Bronze Age example are the bronze idols in figure 62. They were found in a sacrifice pit. They are 10 cm high and were probably fastened to a ship model. The long serpent has a ball in its mouth here, too – the seed being brought to a goddess, who has large gilded eyes, signifying her awareness.

Fig 62. Bronze idols from Fårdal, Jutland, 600 BC

Some later finds depict the snake transporting an entire human body in its mouth.

What is the seed in the mouth of the serpent? Could it be the sun? Or could it be a dead soul? It is probable that some serpents in the Bronze Age transported the sun through the underworld. But the serpents here are most likely carrying a seed representative of the dead soul. The serpent brings the soul to a new life. The sun in the lower world of the short horn has a deer and does not need a serpent. Furthermore, the sun has another symbol on the short horn.

Mother of Life

In the lower world of the short horn, we see a creature with three heads and obviously female genitalia: it is the Mother of Life or Mother Earth in one of her many guises. She is the oldest and most widespread deity in the world. The first farmers in Anatolia worshipped Mother of Earth as early as around 6500 BC. As farming gradually spread throughout Europe, the Goddess took part. Farmers have to be settlers; the soil is their source of life. They are attached to their homeland. Trusting in Mother Earth helped them in their everyday lives. The Goddess was the creator of life and death. She represented the fundamental vitality, the will of life. Faith in Mother Earth gave security, determination, joy and energy to the entire community.

In time and in different cultures, the Goddess acquired different myths and qualities. Different cultures and individuals depicted the Goddess differently. One example is the Scythian drinking horn (figure 28). Another is the bronze idol from Jutland (figure 62). The Goddess had many names, but her common name was Mother Earth. Tacitus mentions that many of the Germanic tribes worshipped her: "By these tribes – taken separately – there is nothing remarkable, except that they in common worship Nerthus, that is to say Mother Earth, and believe that she interferes in men's matters".

The Latin name *Nerthus* was probably an imitation of a Germanic name *Njord-dis*, meaning "nourishing-goddess". In Norse mythology, we find a male god *Njord* ("nourish"). Tacitus describes how the goddess is paraded in a procession or what we would now call a carnival. He also notes that sacrifices to Mother Earth were placed in lakes. This information confirms the many finds of sacrifices in moors.

Quite early on, the Mother of Life gained three aspects, representing the three fundamental forces of life. By the time of the early farmers in Europe, around 5500 BC, her tripartite quality had developed. An ancient symbol for the three forces was three lines, evident in decoration on ceramic grave gifts – a tradition that survived in Europe since 3000 BC. Indeed, three lines was a common symbol in early Balkan culture (Gimbutas 2001), and it was also used by the Angles and many other people. Figure 65 shows some examples from about AD 200, when Funen had a similar culture as the Angles in southern Jutland. The same type of pots and decoration was used later by the English Angles (figure 22).

The idea of a tripartite deity became a part of many European cultures. In Greek mythology, we find the three goddesses of fate called *Moirai*: Clotho ("the spinner") spins the thread of life; Lachesis ("the measurer") gives length to the thread and thus life; and Atropos "the cutter" cuts the thread; thereby ending life. Like deities were known as *Akkas* by the Samic People and as Astaka in India. Similarly, in Norse mythology, we find the three Norns. They live in

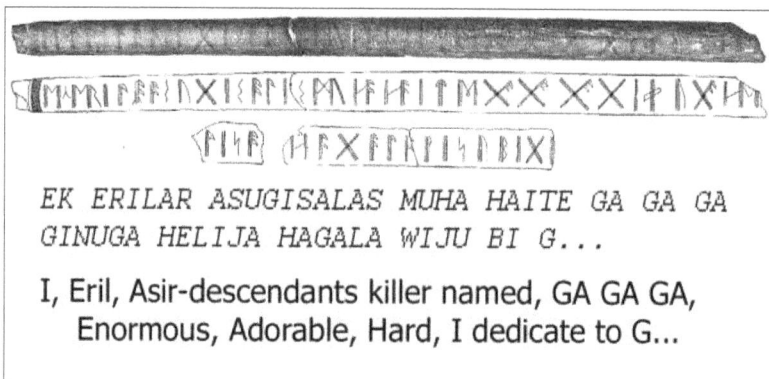

EK ERILAR ASUGISALAS MUHA HAITE GA GA GA
GINUGA HELIJA HAGALA WIJU BI G...

I, Eril, Asir-descendants killer named, GA GA GA,
Enormous, Adorable, Hard, I dedicate to G...

Fig 63. Lance shaft with runic inscription from Kragehul Moor on Funen, AD 400s

the lower world, spinning threads. Their names are *Urd* ("origin"), *Werdandi* ("becoming") and *Skuld* ("necessity"). The three goddesses were depicted as "three mothers" many places in the Germanic and Celtic areas. In Denmark, they are depicted as a three headed goddess as seen on the short horn (figure 57). It may seem strange for us to believe that such a goddesses could determine an entire life at the time of birth. But remember – it was not too long ago that we learned that DNA and genes determine our fate.

.

The many sacrifices of war booty in Jutland and on Funen (AD 200-450) are most probably to the Mother of Life. The lance shaft in figure 63, with a photograph of the lance shaft, followed by a drawing of the runes, a transcription in Latin and, finally, a translation into modern English, is an example of this. The inscription was made by an *eril*, a chieftain. The attackers on southern Funen were Saxons from the south coast of the Baltic, and Saxon chieftains in the AD 400s believed they were descendants of the Aesir Wotan. "GA GA GA" is an invocation of the Earth Goddess whose name began with GA (like the Greek goddess Gaea). Then follow three aspects of Mother Earth. At the end is a dedication to G... but unfortunately the rest of the inscription is missing. Probably the name beginning with G is the earth goddess.

The three-headed goddess (figure 57) on the horn has some attributes. For instance, all three wear precious necklaces. Here, they are referred to as Norns despite a lack of knowledge of what they were called at the time the horn was made.The Norn in the middle with breasts and vagina must be Urd, the producer of the tread of life. The arm to the right holds a thread and that tread ends at the dog of the moon. The moon measures time. The head to the right must be Werdandi, who is giving length to the thread. She also keeps track of time. The arm that holds an axe belongs to Skuld who cuts the thread at the time of death.

Fig 64. Stone heads with three faces from Glejbjerg and Bramminge, southern Jutland. The number "17" on the head from Bramminge is a later carving

Figure 64 shows two stone heads with three faces from the time before the migration of the Angles. Only two of these heads has been found in Denmark, both of them in southern Jutland. One of the faces has a triangle on its forehead, probably the female triangle: she is the birth-giving part of the trinity goddess.

On the short horn, the tree of life is placed beside the Norns, goddesses of life and death. The tree of life is a worldwide symbol of the power of life, the will of life, and has more or less the same meaning as the Mother of Life and sometimes even replaces her. In some cultures, the drink of immortality was produced from the three of life. Ambrosia (`immortality`), the food or drink of the Greek gods was made from a sacred tree. The Scythian drinking horn (figure 28) shows the goddess sitting with her drink of immortality beside the tree of life. In Old Norse mythology, the tree of life is called *Ygg-drasil* (`juice-carrier`) and it had its roots beside the Norns.

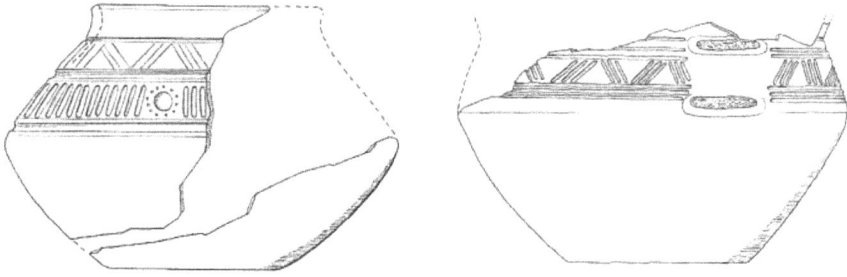

Fig 65. Urns from Funen, around AD 200. (a) Fraude; (b) Alenbækhuse (Albrechtsen 1968)

The Mother of Life places no demands to her worshippers like the Christian God or the Muslim God do. Like other Germanic gods, she does not have rules and principles. She just supports the life of the believer and does not guide her believers through life. The Divine Twins, on the other hand, do guide their believers. The migrating tribes needed a divine guide, which probably explains the popularity of the Divine Twins during the period of the great migrations. Nevertheless, the goddess of bringing new life was still worshipped under the name of Eostra.

The mythology of Mother of Life developed further after the time of the golden horns. Sacrificing in moors, on behalf of the entire tribe, came to an end around AD 450. Instead, the worship of the goddess became a familiar and an indoor matter. In the Migration Age, the goddesses called Hreth and Eostur in England seem to have assumed the roles of the Mother of Life. Hreth fetches the dead soul and Eostur brings it back to life. Then, after the Migration Age, the goddess of life and death, probably called *Freya,* is seen on "guldgubber" and gravestones.

The Twin Gods

The uppermost ring of the short horn features the Twins in the upper world (figures 2 and 57). They are naked because gods do not need clothes. Neither do they have genitalia. They wear horns to demonstrate their power – the horns do not act as weapons for either animals or gods – they signalise the power of creation. Indeed, the power of the Germanic Divine Twins was epitomised by their horns. They were often worshipped with drinking horns.

The twin to the left has a spear, a symbol of his strength, procreativity and courage. He has a wand and a ring in the other hand. This combination is also used in ancient Middle Eastern cultures. The wand is a cutting that will grow and bring life again. The ring is a symbol of the circle of life, regeneration. This twin dies every evening and regenerates every morning. He is young and strong. He grows fast and is the god of growth; the personification of the universal giving force.

This twin was known as Ing by the Angles and other Germanics. The name *Ing* is related to "engender" meaning "beget, procreate" or "engine" meaning "construct".

Above his head are three special stamps. In the middle of the stamp, we have three concentric rings, a symbol of the sun. On the outside we have a three-pointed star, parallel to a three-pronged fork. The three-pointed star represents the three fundamental forces of life. The symbol is widely used. For instance, the three-pronged fork is a symbol of power and life energy in old Indian Shivaism. The god of growth on the horn gives the sun the energy to rise in the morning. He is probably also responsible for the sun getting higher and higher in the spring. He is a god of spring.

The twin to the right has a sickle, a symbol of harvest and the destruction of living organisms. He is the god of harvest and a god of autumn. But he is also a god of death, known by some people as the Man with the Scythe. On the other hand, he has a pointer, which is to show us he is the leader and knows the way, particularly the way through the world of the dead. He also takes care of the sun as it sets in the afternoon and at night. He is the personification of the receiving universal force.

On top of his head is his special stamp. We find the same stamp three times with the same god on the ring of the worker (see figure 57). The stamp is a sun with a four-pointed star, suggesting a cross, which is a traditional symbol of the earth or land, with the four world directions. The god of harvest is also the god of wealth, lord of the earth.

The short horn also features the worker (figure 57). Indeed, the placing of this ring is the same as the worker's ring on the long horn but, interestingly, there is no worker here. The god of harvest holds a line, which ends at the muzzle of a horse. But the line is not fastened to the horse. Rather it signifies that the god controls the horse. The horse has a saddle and a very short horn, perhaps again a symbol of fertility. The horse is a symbol of the sky. A horse drawing the celestial sphere is well known from ancient Indian Sanskrit literature. It is also mentioned several times in Old Norse literature. For instance, the poem *Vaftrudnesmal* [the Song of Vavtrudner]:

Skinfaxe is he
Sky high he raises
Day at **D**awn
The best **H**orse
For the **H**eroes

Shining is the **M**ane of the **M**are
Hrimfaxe is he
High he raises
Night for **n**ourishing gods
Foam in the morning
Falls from the muzzle
As **D**ew falls **D**own

The kind of Norse alliterative metre is called *ljodahattr;* the alliteration is marked in bold. Other Norse poems make it clear that the two horses were steered by two different gods. The metal beaker from the AD 500s in figure 87 depicts the twin gods having a horse each. We can assume that the horse we see with the harvest god is the one later called Hrimfaxe.

Below and above the horse we find two stamps, which resemble the sun symbol in the upper rings. The eight-pointed star still symbolises the sky, but the little balls at the end of the eight points are not present here: the sky, not the movement of the sun in eight eikts, is in focus. This star is probably a symbol for the night sky in accordance with the horse Hrimfaxe, who raised the night sky. The moon dogs and the symbols of the full moon and new moon contribute to this assumption. The sky-horse is the wind, bringing all kinds of weather and climate: cold, hot, rain, snow, storm, hoarfrost and so on. This ring is the ring of the worker, corresponding to the worker ring on the long horn, but here the subject is the outside forces that influence a farmer's life. Remember, the primary force, the god of harvest hopefully lived in the worker.

Below the sickle, on the worker ring, we find an ornament called a running spiral, which has been used worldwide. It is the most common ornament of the Nordic Bronze Age. The Greek meander is also a running spiral. Most likely, it is a symbol of Time. Time is a repeating pattern of life. Whether it be the repetition of days, months or years, it can be illustrated with repeating spirals. The god of harvest also keeps track of Time and he has moon dogs to help him. The running spiral is seen several times on the short horn as it spirals upwards in the direction of the life of the individual.

Moon dogs are again a feature of the ring of the worker. Above is the sign of the earth, because the moon is connected to the cultivation of the earth. We recognise the dog of the waxing moon to the left. Just like in the ring of heaven his tail imitates the shape of the waxing moon and he is situated between the signs of the new moon and the full moon. This dog represents the giving force of life and it jumps higher than the other dog, which represents the receiving force. Moon phases were essential for farming activities and other activities of the Germanics. The farmers kept track of the waxing moon and the waning moon.

The short horn describes human life, and animals play an important role in human life as a food source. These animals are generated by hidden natural forces of divine character. The Divine Twins were believed to be vital for the growth and exploitation of animals. But the consumption of animals as a food source could be perceived as a sacrifice to the gods. Like all other ancient people, the Germanics sacrificed animals. The flesh of the victim was normally consumed by the participants of the ritual as a form of communion with the deity. If the Divine Twins were invoked, the participants became their abode. From that point of view, the many punctured animals on the short horn could be seen as sacrificial animals.

Half of the punctured creatures are fish, which all look the same and were probably stamped. The fish move upwards on the horn, perhaps denoting the direction of human life. Fish seem to have constituted a substantial part of the diet of people in the area where the short horn was made. Indeed, that area, the west coast of southern Jutland and Holstein, had good fishing. The ring of the dead soul has no fish, because the dead soul cannot ascent to the next ring of heaven.

The remaining animals are mammals or birds. Note that human beings only appear on the ring of the leader and of the child and that neither of these rings have mammals or birds. Perhaps indicating that mammals and birds were always sacrificed to the gods.

The four mythic figures on the ring of the worker were all essential for farming. Most of the figures on the short horn belong to the spiritual world – and, essentially, the spiritual world is the spiritual life inside man. Deities and myths belong to the collective spiritual world.

The Two Warriors

In the ring of heaven on the short horn (figures 2 and 57) are two almost identical warriors, placed beside each other on the concave side of the horn, above the archer and the deer. The loins of the warriors protrude up from the surface of the horn. Two gold chains must have been fastened here. A third chain was probably fastened to the narrow end of the horn and the three chains met in a ring. This arrangement made it possible to hang up the horn even if it was full and is known from other archaeological finds.

The sword was an expensive weapon and was reserved for chieftains. The warriors have neck rings of gold. We know from grave finds that precious neck rings were used by the elite as a symbol of high rank. The similarity of the warriors tells us that they are depictions of the Divine Twins. However, there are a few differences: the decorations on the shields differ in the shape and number of star points. One has 17 points, while the other has 10. Paulli's drawing is very careful in many ways but we cannot rely on his number of points. Most likely, there were 15 and 9; thereby, corresponding to the number of runes in the upper and lower world.

Another slight difference can be found in the two stamps beside the warriors. The stamps consist of a ring surrounded by eight pairs of tentacles. One of the rings contains two smaller rings probably indicating light. The other ring is empty indicating darkness. The symbol with pairs of tentacles probably stands for attention, threatening and defence. It resembles the *ægishjalmr* symbol in figure 68, which has a similar meaning. Similar symbols appear in other places on the horn and are referred to here as the "defence symbol".

The decoration on their shields and the defence symbols beside the warriors tell us that one of them guides and protects during the day and is visible in life, whereas the other warrior guides and protects at night and in the spiritual world. However, they complement each other like the Divine Twins and are, indeed, personifications of the Divine Twins, considered to have a vital function for the tribe.

The two warriors have weapons and, therefore, they cannot be gods for gods do not need weapons. Neither do they wear clothes, so they are not normal living humans. The two warriors are protective spirits; most probably heroic ancestors of the tribe living in the spiritual world. It is doubtful that these warriors ever lived, rather their heroic tradition lived. Most societies claim to descend from heroic ancestors. A common ancestor defines an ethnic group. When the group pays attention to its ancestors and honours them with rituals, it strengthens the solidarity and the self-confidence of the group. If the ancestors are heroes, it gives the descendants prestige and self-esteem. Kings are very often thought to descend from gods. The original Germanic society was a tribal society and each tribe had their own ancestors.

Stamps with defensive symbols are also found on some of the other rings of the horn. For instance, on the ring of the leader is a defensive symbol of four pairs of tentacles above the armed twin in the human wheel. The stamp forms a cross with the cross probably referring to the land of the tribe. The stamp is placed near the vigorous Divine Twin "Ing", indicating that his force helps defend the tribe.

Two other defensive symbols of the same kind are placed in the ring of the leader. The double animal with a head at both ends has been a common symbol in northern Europe since the Bronze Age. It is clearly a representation of the Divine Twins. The animals here could be watch dogs, suggesting that the leader's attention goes in all directions and he is ready to face all challenges. The stamp at the middle of the double animal is a cross meaning the land, the residence of the tribe. The two defence symbols near the heads mean defending the land.

Similarly, there are defence symbols on the ring of the child, which features a young archer. Like the other archers on the horns, the archer is not trying to hit anything. The symbol means that the young man is attentive. It is difficult to explain the symbol drawing his attention – it seems to be the body or the outspread skin of a sacrificed boar. On the top, we see the head of a mysterious female, presumably the individual to whom the sacrifice is directed. The many nearby cross stamps indicate that the subject here is the attention to and defence of the tribe and land. The young man is ready to sacrifice his energy and life to the tribe as symbolised by the female head. For the Germanic tribes, lineage was bound to the mother. The Danish word *kone* (wife) has the same root as the old Norse *kyn* (kin). The female head does not need to be his mother or a female ancestor. It is just a general symbol of the ethnic group. It is evident from the use of defence symbols that the long horn is a description of the outlook on life in tribal society.

Many ancient people worshipped the Divine Twins and they believed their ancestors were twins. The Romans descended from twins Romus (Romulus is a secondary form) and Remus. Some authors believe that a biological pair of twins was considered divine and later became heroic ancestors. This theory does not give much sense as biological twins occur often and they cannot all be ancestors.

All the ancestors we know of in Germanic tribes are twins. Donald Ward gives many examples of these pairs of ancestors and each pair has evolved from the mythological Divine Twins (Ward 1968).

One typical example of a Germanic tribe with ancestor twins is the Longobards ("long axes"). The origin of the Langobards is told by several ancient writers. The Vinnilers in Scandinavia suffered from a famine and some of them emigrated to Scoringa. The leaders of the immigrants were a pair of brothers Ebor ("wild boar") and Agio ("tusk of a boar"), and their mother Gambara ("mother of bearing", cf English "gammer" means "old mother"). The brothers were superior in strength and their mother had prophetic powers. When they came to Scoringa, they met the Vandals (migrates) and had to fight them. At this point, Gambara turned to Frea, mistress of Godan, for help. After their victory, the Vinniler called themselves Langobards.

It is fairly clear that the Vinnilers worshipped the mother of life and the Divine Twins. These were the three most important Germanic gods. In Old Norse literature, they were called *Vanir* (beautiful, fair), and it is possibly the name Vinniler stems from the name Vanir, though there are three alternative explanations of the legend. It is possible that when the Vinniler left Scandinavia, they attributed the qualities of their gods to some persons within the tribe. These persons were considered the mortal incarnations of the gods. Another possibility is that the entire legend was constructed many years later by the Langobards, who needed godlike ancestors.

A third – and most probably – possibility is that the Vinniler represented the Divine Twins in their boar tusks. A large number of boar brooches have been found along the Elbe River, where the Langobards lived. In the original legend, the leaders of the Vinnilers were probably the Divine Twins with boar names together with the mother of life. Many years later, the oral legend changed, because the boar names were then understood as names of historic persons.

There are several finds of boar crested helmets from Sweden and England, and the helmets are described in old literature. In fact, the

Fig 66. Boar-crested helmet from Benty Grange in Derbyshire (Mercia), AD 600s

two warriors are standing on boar tusks on the helmet from Sutton Hoo (figure 4).

The boar in figure 66 is placed on top of a corroded helmet found in a grave at the Benty Grange Farm. The decoration of the boar is made from gilded silver and copper. The use of helmets with boar symbols in England is probably due to the influence from Sweden, where the boar was a symbol of the young warrior god Frey/Ing. The boar is strong and powerful and protects his family and is a good symbol for the god Ing. Similar helmets to the Sutton Hoo helmet have been found in burial grounds from around AD 600 in the Swedish district of Vendel.

The Yule Boar is an old tradition in England connected to Ing. The custom can still be seen today at Queen's College, Oxford. Here, the head of a boar is paraded annually on 17th December on a silver platter during a customary dinner. An orange is placed in the mouth of the boar, probable with the same symbolism as the serpent with the seed on the short horn (figure 57). The orange and the seed are symbols of the Sun, which has been brought up from the underworld. From Old Norse literature, we know that Frey's sacred animal was the boar, and it was sacrificed at his Yule festival.

Following the Viking Age tradition, Swein Forkbeard, son of the deceased Danish king, invited all the chieftains to a Yule party in AD 980. He could not take the royal throne before drinking the heritage beer after his father. A yule boar was slaughtered at the party and the participants made promises by laying their hand on the boar. The Christian Swein Forkbeard promised that within three years he would come with his army to England and kill king Ethelred (known as "Ethelred the Unready") or drive him away. Everybody had to drink a toast to it. Notably, Swein Forkbeard did become king of England – but not until AD 1013.

According to the legend, the Langobards had to fight another migrating tribe, the Vandals. The leaders of the Vandals were two young brothers, Ambri (beam) and Assi (pillar). Indeed, there were Vandal tribes known as *Ambrones* and *Assipitti*. Other Vandals are said to have been led by a pair of youths, Raos (pole) and Raptos (post), whose names indicate the Vandals worshipped the Divine Twins as two poles. The Divine Twins were the real leaders of the tribe. The legend of the young human brothers is a secondary construction.

In the legend of Hengist and Horsa (see the chapter entitle "The Jutes"), two brothers, ancestors of the Royal House of Kent, led the first invasion. From Snorre's *Ynglinga Saga,* we learn that the Swedish royal family, the Ynglingar, considered themselves descendants of Frey and Njord.

Another example of how a religious myth is reconstructed as heroic legend is found in Old Indian tradition, the Sun Maiden is liberated every morning from darkness by the Divine Twins. In Greek tradition, the king of Athens abducted Helena from Sparta, but Castor and Polydeukes brought her back. The beautiful Helena was abducted several times – one of which famously caused the Trojan War. It has been proposed that, in reality, it was an idol of the goddess Helena that was abducted. It makes sense given the preciousness of such idol and that possessing it imbued power.

When the tribal communities migrated, they created a leading warrior class. Warriors need heroic legends not religious myths. The oral legends were passed on for generations and that is what we have today. The Greek Heroic Age covers the period from the Trojan War (around 1200 BC) until the legends were transcribed in *the Iliad* around 700 BC. During the Heroic Age, society was dominated by small warlords and pirates. The heroic legends and mythology of many gods fighting each other are characteristic of such a society. A similar development took place in the Germanic Age and at the beginning of the Viking Age, where the tribal society crumbled and a society of small warlords and pirates was left. Indeed, the Viking Age and its mythology has much in common with that of the Greek heroic age.

Stamps

The short horn has many complex symbols made using a stamp technique. Most have been examined here. The long horn has only simple punctured figures. The stamp technique appeared around AD 400; the time of which the short horn must have been made. The most remarkable stamp that occurs repeatedly on the short horn is an eight-pointed star encircling three concentric rings. As discussed earlier, this stamp is the "sun symbol" (see the section entitled "The Twin Gods").

The sun symbols do not have the same number of points in Paulli's drawing (figures 57 and 67); some of them are lacking the small balls, but in another drawing, by Frost (1774), they all look the same and have eight points. There are nine sun symbols in the part of the horn representing the underworld and fifteen sun symbols in that

Fig 67. The two uppermost rings of the short horn with the 24 sun symbols marked

representing the upper world, making 24 sun symbols altogether – the same number of runes in the older runic alphabet (figure 6). Germanics and other people divided both heaven and the sun's movement into eight parts. Consequently, day and night was divided into eight parts. These parts were called *eikts* (tides) in Icelandic.

The 24 runes of the runic alphabet represented the life of the sun for a night and a day. The sequence of runes was also divided into eight parts with three runes in each eikt. In Antiquity, night preceded day and consequently the alphabet started at sundown in the northwest (figure 6). The first three eikts, with nine runes, belonged to the night, when the sun was in the lower world. The nine runes, divided into three eikts, appear as sun symbols in the lower world in figure 67, marked in blue. The next five eikts, with fifteen runes, belonged to the day, when the sun was in the upper world. The 15 day runes appear as sun symbols in the upper world in figure 67, marked in yellow.

The long horn was made around AD 20 and runes were not invented at that time. Nevertheless, the long horn (figure 43) is punctured 24

Fig 68. Ægishjalmr

times: nine times in the first ring and fifteen times in the second ring. These triangular punctures differ greatly from the style of the horn and must be a later addition. Whoever was responsible, probably interpreted the first ring of the long horn as the lower world and the second ring as the upper world.

The Icelandic *Galdrabok* ("Book of Magic") from AD 1550 has preserved some of the old Germanic magical practice (Flowers 1989): magical symbols with runes. Many of the symbols are variations on the so called *ægishjalmr* (figure 68). The first part *ægis* is Indo-European in origin *aig* ("to move suddenly"). The Greek *aigis* ("frightening", "awe") was the name of Pallas Athene's shield. The goddess did not need a shield for protection, only for scaring. The Aegean Sea is the scary sea. The Old Norse sea god *Ægir* was "the frightening one". Old Norse *ægr* or *ygr* means "terrible". The last part *hjalmr* means "cover". The same root is found in the English word *helmet*. So *ægishjalmr* means "scary cover". In fact, Germanic magical practice tells us that if you carry the symbol *ægishjalmr*,

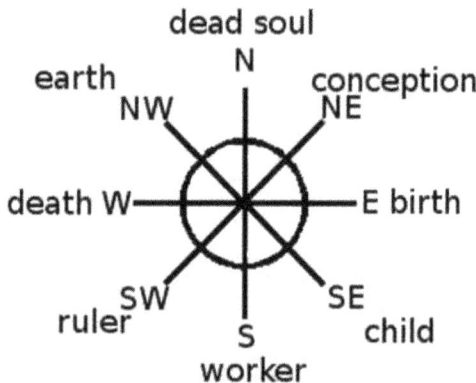

Fig 69. The human life cycle

your enemies will fear you, your courage will be strengthened and you will be protected against all evil.

Magical runic symbols use many three-pronged forks, indicating that the fork symbolises an eikt with three runes. Sometimes, the magical symbol includes only part of the eikt in the ægishjalmr (figure 68). The different eikts correspond to different parts of the life cycle. Primarily, this cycle represents the life of the sun during a night and a day. However, the eikts become an allegory of the human life cycle, too. Note the correlation between the eight eikts and the eight phases of human life in figure 69. Some of the phases correspond to the rings of the Gold Horns with birth naturally belonging in the east, where the sun is born, and death in the west, where the sun sets.

The Runic Alphabet

The 24 runes of the Germanic runic alphabet always occur in the same sequence, with the single rune symbol always taking approximately the same form (figure 6). This tells us that the alphabet was invented by a definite person at a definite time and in a definite place, probably around AD 150. The invention was not an arbitrary idea from a single originator. It was certainly based on the Germanic outlook on life. Runes were designed for inscribing in wood. The word "write" comes from the old English word *writan* ("to inscribe").

Many of the preserved inscriptions were made by erils, and most probable the runic alphabet was invented by an eril who was chieftain of the tribe that preserved the long horn. The distribution of all runic inscriptions suggests that the runic alphabet was invented in Slesvig-Holstein, though the North Frisian Islands and the continental coast in front of them are more probable. For convenience, this area is called Ambronia here, because of the Ambrones, who, in 114 BC, marched south and fought the Romans with the Kimbrians and others. The Old English poem *Widsith* notes a tribe called the Ymbri. One of the North Frisian Islands is called Amrum. The Greek *brotos* means "mortal" and the Greek *ambrotos* means "immortal". The meaning of the tribe name Ambrones could very well be "the immortals".

In Ambronia, we find the place names Meldorf and Gallehus, where North Alpine letters were found, and it is almost certain that the common theory of the runes being inspired by the North Alpine letters holds true. After all, a chieftain in Ambronia, named HLEWAGASTICh and who knew the runes made a long inscription on the short horn. The stamps on the horns show that the owners new the deeper meaning of the runes very well. Runic stone inscriptions in pre-Christian England are found mostly in the Anglian areas, north of the Thames, indicating that the migrants from southern Jutland were acquainted with runes.

In Roman times, Ambronia was well populated. The habitable land, which was larger than today because sea level was 2m lower and considerable areas are now covered by drift-sand, had many advantages: marsh and meadows for animals; fishing and waterfowl. The inhabitants controlled the north-south traffic that always passed between the islands and the continent. Travellers would stay for a night in harbours such as Wyk on the island of Föhr and they had to pay. The people in Ambronia could build boats and raid other tribes. Indeed, some one runic symbol (Path) shows a ship with high stem (figure 74).

The power held by these people is evident in the fortification rings, dating from the AD 000s, near Gallehus (see the chapter on the origin of the long horn). Some archaeologists believe that the three ring walls (Trælbanke, Achsumburg and Tinnumburg) in Ambronia were built by the Angles who also built the contemporaneous Olger Dike (figure 7). Some Angles came from northern Germany in the AD 000s and invaded the eastern part of Istathe Syssel, but it is likely that another ethnic group established themselves on the west coast by that time. All the Germanic ethnic groups near the North Sea had a similar material culture and god, Ing, and in some sense could be called Angles. When they arrived in England, in the AD 400s, they were all called Angles.

The tribes in Amnronia could be Chaucis. It is possible that a Chauci chieftain moved to this area at some point with the long horn. After AD 200, the Chauci are no longer mention. Some of them were called Saxons, and the tribe in Ambronia may have had another name. Ptolemy may be helpful here: in AD 130, he located some islands called "alokiai nesoi" at the site of the North Frisian Islands. The main town on the island of Föhr is called *Alkersum* ("Home of the sacred place"), which is reminiscent of the rune *Alchi* ("guiding gods") (figure 74), and perhaps offers a hint at the tribe's name.

The runes received names at the time they were invented. These names were written down in a few locations much later, each varying a little. The best source is the Anglo-Saxon runic poem, first written down in the ninth century. Only copies survive today. The Gothic letters used in the fourth century by Wulfila had names, which resonate with the rune names and confirm some of the rune names. It is worth mentioning that Old Norse literature also has rune names, but they belong to the runic alphabet used in the Viking Age. This alphabet had only 16 runes and was based on another outlook on life, so it is not relevant here.

The form of the runes, their names and sequence in the alphabet has until now been a mystery. However, there is a way to solve the mystery. Placing the runic alphabet (figure 6) within the human life-cycle, which consists of eight eikts (figure 69), corresponding to the eight parts of the night and day cycle of the sun, beginning with the f rune, in the northwest eikt means the rest of the runes fall into place as we see in figure 6. Remember, for the Germanic people the day started at sundown and night was before day. This system is still in use in some cultures today.

To explain the rune symbols and the rune names in relation to their position in the cycle, starting with the runes in the east, which, according to figure 69, is the birth phase of the human life-cycle. Figure 70 (below) shows the three runes in the east. The phonetic value of each rune is noted underneath that runic symbol, followed by the rune-name from the Anglo-Saxon rune poem and, finally, a suggestion for the meaning of the original rune name.

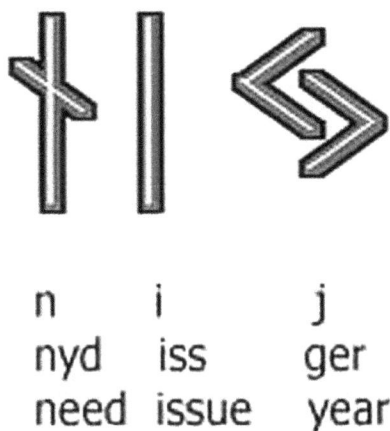

n	i	j
nyd	iss	ger
need	issue	year

Fig 70. Runes in the east connected to the birth of man

The rune symbols in figure 70 are understandable because we know, from the short horn, how the three Norns were connected to birth. Thus, according to this theory, the Norn in the middle, who produces the thread, corresponds to the i rune – the runic symbol being a tread. The Norn to the right measures the tread with the corresponding j rune being perhaps two hands or two dividers measuring the thread. The Norn, to the left, cuts the thread and the n rune perfectly illustrates this action.

The bottom line in figure 70 contains suggestions for the meanings of the original rune names. There is no expectation for an English word to have the same meaning as an ancient Germanic rune name. We need to bear in mind that these names were made 700 years before the runic names from the Anglo-Saxon rune poem. The language had changed and some of the rune names must have changed, too. There might be similar words in other Germanic languages for some of the rune names but not in English.

The sources have different rune names for the i rune: *is, iiz, iss*. The

Indo-European root "is" means "out" as does the Latin *ex;* the Greek *is-thmo* means "out-movement", the French *issir*, "to go out" and English "issue" means "offspring". The rune name is related to the birth-giving goddess. The Egyptian mother of life, Ast, was called *Isis* ("emitter") by the Greeks. The meaning of the i rune name was probably "product" or "issue".

The name of the j rune is "year". Years come from the universal giving force at the birth and are measured by the Norn to the right. The English word "need" probably has the same root as the original n rune name. We have words with the same root in other Germanic languages, meaning "necessity" or "trouble". The Norn to the left represents need. She is holding back. She is the universal receiving force in connection to birth. The belief that the Norns can foresee a human life at the time of birth may seem strange to modern man. But it is the equivalent of our belief that heritage or DNA can foresee life.

The next chapter examines the whole runic alphabet, revealing something about the Germanic view of human life as it does. At the core of Germanic life was freedom. Unlike Judaism, Christianity and Islam, there were no moral rules. Nothing was absolutely good or bad. There were no principles that could be broken, not even your own ones. The runes explain that there are three forces in life. Which of the three depends best on the situation. You have to use the available information to choose the right path. This includes taking other people's intentions into consideration. You might say the Germanic individual was pragmatic but he was not spineless or inconsiderate. He was loyal to his family and his ethnic group as it was his only security.

The Human Life Cycle

We have seen that the rune symbols and the rune names seem to be connected to the Germanic outlook on life. But what about the rest of the runic alphabet and the human life cycle as viewed by the Germanics. The runic alphabet tells the story of human life in a different way to the Golden Horns, but the fundamental ideas are the same.

The first eikt in the northwest represents the earth, and here it means both minerals and biological material. The earth is where we end our life and from where all life comes. *Ur* in Norwegian means the original rock and gravel without soil or plants. The u rune depicts a rock. The f rune represents the giving force of the earth. Feoh can be interpreted as "cattle", but "yield" is more representative of the giving force of the earth. The two secondary strokes of the f rune probably mean vegetation. The th rune shows a thorn, which represents the receiving force of the earth. Whether the thorn sits on a plant or a stone, it is able to cut and take your blood.

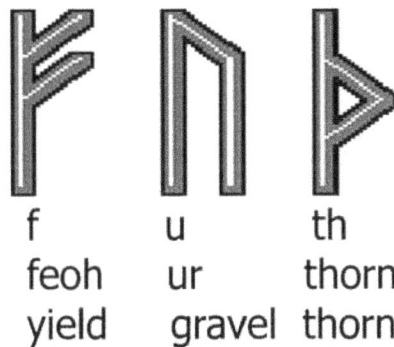

Fig 71. Runes in the northwest connected to the earth

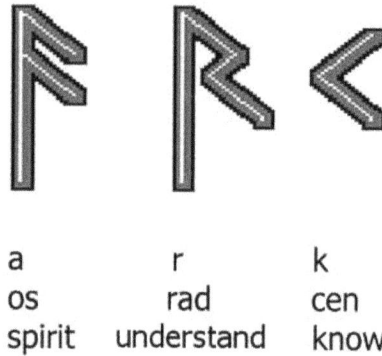

a   r   k
os   rad   cen
spirit understand know

Fig 72. Runes in the north connected to the dead spirit

The r rune symbol probably represents the human head. Here, we find the thoughts and ideas that constitute our inner spiritual life. *Rad* could mean "interpret, advice or understand". Most probably the latter. The old English word *rædan* means "to interpret". The k rune could be a speaking mouth. This is the giving force of the spirit. In Old Norse *cen* means know. The a rune symbol seems to be a hollow phenomenon coming from above, probably representing an invisible spirit. *Os* has the same root as *asir* ("elevated, raised"), the name of the gods in Old Norse mythology. *Os* could also mean spirit. The receiving force of the spirit is invisible, listening and observing.

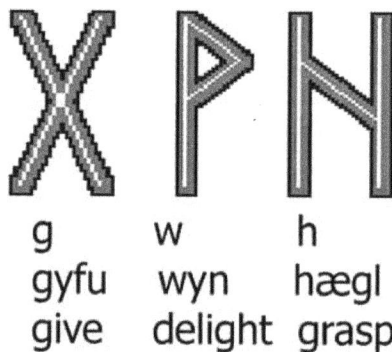

g   w   h
gyfu wyn hægl
give delight grasp

Fig 73. Runes in the northeast connected to conception

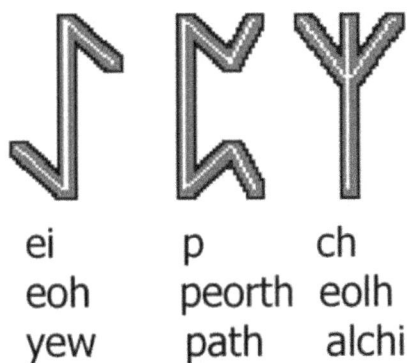

ei   p   ch
eoh   peorth eolh
yew   path   alchi

Fig 74. Runes in the southeast connected to the child

Most of all, the w rune symbol resembles a flag, indicating a party. *Wyn* is preserved in the German *wonne* ("delight"). The h rune probably illustrates sexual intercourse. The Norse name of this rune, *hagal* probably means "to hock". Words such as *hægl,* meaning "grasp", are preserved in some Germanic languages. This rune is the giving force of conception, the male force. The g rune symbol is more difficult to explain. More likely, it is a gift, such as a baby in swaddling.

As the east runes were examined already (figure 70), the south east runes will be addressed here (figure 74). The development and education of the child is compared to a journey or path. The p rune probably illustrates a ship with high sterns. *Alchi* is the name of the Divine Twins (as we will see later). The *ch* sound in *alchi* is preserved in the German *dich*. The ch rune name does not begin with ch, because there was no Germanic word beginning with the ch sound. It is possible that the ch rune is a fast growing tree, but more likely it is a symbol of the three universal forces: the will to live and the Divine Twins. The same symbol is seen as the three-pronged forks of the *ægishjalmr* (figure 68). Yew is a slow growing tree. The ei rune shows a tree with roots, of which neither the

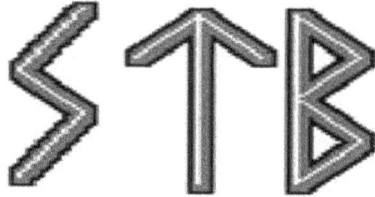

s	t	b
sigel	tir	beorc
seek	procreate	gather

75. Runes in the south connected to the worker

branches nor the roots grow. This rune is the receiving force of the child. The child grows slowly and sticks to its roots.

Tir means bull and the bull has always been the emblem of procreative power. This runic symbol most probable depicts an erect penis, a symbol of creative power. The s rune represents the giving force of the worker. The zigzag movement demonstrates energy and activity. The b rune represents the receiving force of the worker. The name *beorc* is similar to the Danish *bjærge*, meaning "save or

e	m	l
eh	man	lagu
horse	urge	law

Fig 76. Runes in the southwest connected to the ruler

gather". The b rune probably symbolises two piles of gathered harvest. When we look at figure 67, we find the three sun symbols representing these three runes exactly on top of the bull.

The original meaning of the word *man* was "talk". In some modern Germanic languages, *man* means "urge". In Sanskrit legends, *Manu* was ancestor of men. The m rune symbol looks like a folding chair. Chairs like that were used as thrones for Germanic kings and other ancient people. The e rune could be accepted as a picture of a horse, which is a symbol of the giving force of the ruler. Chieftains had to travel on horseback to lead warriors or control subjects in different areas. Law represents the receiving force of the ruler. When the king exercised his power as a judge, he sat and received people. He would hold a staff to emphasise his power. The l rune symbol may be such a staff.

Death is the time when the soul leaves the body. The butterfly leaving the cocoon is a common symbol for this process, and the d rune is indeed a butterfly. On the left side, we find the giving force of death *Ing*. Ing, as we have seen, is the giving twin of the two Divine Twins, who dies every sunset and is born every sunrise (we will return to him again later). He is a symbol of the reincarnation that the deceased can expect probably in his own family. The ng rune probably shows a star. *Othel* means "inheritance or nobility". Here, on the right side, is no reincarnation. The heirs in the family will profit from the deceased. The symbol here is a star setting on the horizon. It is interesting that the last letter symbol in the rune alphabet seems to be the same as the last letter symbol *omega* in the Greek alphabet.

The 24 letters of the runic alphabet describe the whole life cycle of the individual. The letters of the alphabet also make it possible to express everything in life. This is by no means exceptional for the

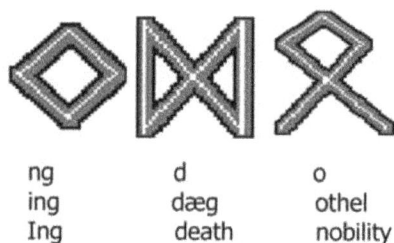

ng	d	o
ing	dæg	othel
Ing	death	nobility

Fig 77. Runes in the west connected to death

runic alphabet. The expression "alpha to omega" – and even the contemporary "a to z" – means everything in life because it represents the entire Greek alphabet. The first alphabet in the world was from *Ugarit*, and how it described the Ugaritic view of life has been examined (Rasmussen 1997).

The runes were meant for inscriptions. With the inscribed object then gaining the spiritual qualities of the inscription. The runic symbol alone would do as it is an abbreviation of the rune name. In this way, rune symbols could be used for magic. There are several examples of rune magic from archaeology as well as from Norse literature. In the *Poetic Edda Sigrdrifumal,* a Valkyrie teaches Sigurd some rune magic. For example, she tells him that a midwife should draw b runes (meaning "save") on her palms at a delivery.

Runes are used as abbreviations on some sceattas that show a person raising a spear. They are found in England and were probably minted in a trade centre such as Ipswich in the AD 600s. A contemporary literature review has not revealed a careful study of these sceattas. The person on the sceatta (figure 78) is probably the god Ing. Like the god with a spear and a ring on the Golden Horn (figure 2), he is naked and without genitalia. He is stabbed to death because his fate is to die every night. A similar incident is depicted on some gold bracteates.

Fig 78. Sceatta found near Ipswich, East Anglia, ca. AD 700 (Rickfors)

The b rune, at the top, means "save" or "acquire". The symbol shows two piles of merchandise and is a reasonable description of a trade and craft centre. The three dots refer to the three forces of life and are an introduction to the following three runes. The b rune is common for this kind of sceattas, but the following three runes do not always accompany it on sceattas. When runes were uses for foreshadowing, three rune sticks were picked up. The e rune means "horse" or "power of the ruler" in its broad sense. The p rune means "path" or "travelling" in its broad sense. The last rune is the Anglo Saxon *os,* corresponding to the old a rune and meaning "spirit" or "being enlightened" in its broad sense. The three runes seem to be a good recommendation for a centre of trade.

An alphabet, which pictured life would have been held in high regard among the Germanic tribes. That is the reason the runic alphabet spread and continued in use, almost unchanged, for centuries. Another advantage of having an alphabet with a meaningful sequence of letters is that it makes it easier to learn and remember. Some of the runes were not really necessary for writing. The new perception of life in the Viking Age caused the introduction of another runic alphabet.

The Germanic Calendar

A great number of marks were found on the long horn. They were acute angles scratched into the surface, which are not seen on the drawing in figure 43. They are visible in Ole Worm's original drawing, but he recorded that he did not draw the exact number of marks. Instead, he made a uniform ornamentation of the angles. However, Jørgen Sorterup had the horn in his hands in AD 1722, when he examined the marks carefully. From his essay on them, we know where the marks were placed (Oxenstierna 1956). The angle marks were placed in groups between the figures and the number of marks in each group seems to have been determined by the free space between the figures. The total number of marks in a ring is more interesting. It is remarkable that the numbers of angle marks in a ring are multiples of 24. The rings are numbered from the bottom.

Ring 1 above and Ring 2 below together: 4 multiples of 24 angle marks.
Ring 2 above: One group of 24 angle marks. One group of 2 multiplies of 24 angle marks.
Ring 3 below: 18 angle marks, the last one was horizontal as a stop mark.
Ring 3 above: 2 multiplies of 24 angle marks. 18 sun marks.
Ring 4: 5 multiplies of 24 angle marks.
Ring 5: 54 angle marks. 4 sun marks.
Ring 6: No marks
Ring 7: 7 multiplies of 24 angle marks.

Ring 3 below and ring 5 are peculiar. When taken together, they amount to 72 marks, which is equal to 3 multiplies of 24 marks. The total number of angle marks on the horn was 24 multiplies of 24 marks.

The number 24 may have something to do with the calendar. Germanic tribes – like most ancient people – followed a moon calendar. The Germanics believed that the movement of the sun was controlled by the moon. This idea is illustrated in figures 2 and 61, where the sun deer is hunted by two moon dogs. In the summer, the sun is high up in the sky and in the winter it is low; the moon follows the sun in this movement. The first date of the year is rather easy to determine. At midsummer the site of the sunset stops moving north. After midsummer, you have to wait for the first new moon to show up after sunset. The first date of the year starts at this sunset. Every date starts with a sunset. A new month starts when a new moon arrives.

For the Germanics, the night of the new moon and the night of the full moon were important milestones that divided life into stages, and they were celebrated as festivals. The night of the full moon was used for outdoor gatherings of the community with bonfires. The night of the new moon was used for sacrifices to the ancestors and deities. The phases between the festivals – the waxing moon and the waning moon – had different traits, connected to the giving and the receiving forces, respectively. Several cultures have rules for farming activities and sexual activities within the two phases of the moon. Caesar tells us that Germanic tribes decided warfare depending on the moon phase.

The Venerable Bede, a Northumbrian monk in his *The Reckoning of Time,* from around AD 720, has described the heathen English calendar. As there is very little further information available about the Germanic calendar, his remarks are quoted here translated from Latin by Wallis (1999):

> The first month, which in Latin is called January, is *Giuli*; February is called *Solmonath*; March *Hrethmonath*; April *Eosturmonath*: May *Thrimilchi*; June *Litha*; July also *Litha*;

August *Weodmonath*; September *Halegmonath*; October *Winterfilleth*; November *Blodmonath*; December *Giuli*, the same name by which January is called. They began the year on the 8th kalends of January (25 December), when we celebrate the birth of the Lord. That very night, which we hold so sacred, they used to call by the heathen word *Modranecht,* that is "mother's night", because of the ceremonies they enacted all that night.

Whenever it was a common year, they gave three lunar months to each season. When an embolismic year occurred (that is, one of 13 lunar months) they assigned the extra month to summer, so that three months together bore the name "*Litha*"; hence they called the year "*Thrilith*". It had four summer months, with the usual three for the other seasons. But originally, they divided the year as a whole into two seasons, summer and winter, assigning the six months in which the days are longer than the nights to summer, and the other six to winter. Hence they called the month in which the winter season began "*Winter filleth*", a name made up from "winter" and "full Moon", because the winter began on the full Moon of that month.

Nor is it irrelevant if we take the trouble to translate the names of the other months. The months of *Giuli* derive their name from the day when the sun turns back to increase because one of these months precedes this day and the other follows. *Solmonath* can be called "month of cakes", which they offered to their gods in that month. *Hrethmonath* is named for their goddess *Hretha*, to whom they sacrificed at this time. *Eosturmonath* has a name which is now translated "Paschal month", and which was once called after a goddess of theirs named *Eostur*, in whose honour feasts were celebrated in that month. Now they designate that Paschal season by her name, calling the joys of the new rite by the time-honoured name of the old observance. *Thrimilchi* was so called because in that month the cattle were milked three times a day; such at one time, was the fertility of Britain or Germany, from whence the English nation came to Britain. *Litha* means "gentle" or "navigable", because in both these months the calm breezes are gentle, and they were wont to sail upon the smooth sea. *Weodmonath* means "month of tares", for they are very plentiful then. *Halegmonath* means "month of sacred rites". *Winterfilleth* can be called by the invented composite name "winter-full". *Blodmonath* is "month of immolations", for then the cattle which were to be slaughtered were consecrated for their gods. Good Jesu, thanks to be thee, who hast turned us away from these vanities and given us grace to offer to thee the sacrifice of praise.

To offer a commentary on Bede's text: it is doubtful that *Litha* means gentle and has anything to do with the sea. The Danish word *lide* can mean "suffer", "deteriorate", "being trustworthy", "moving" or "to relent". *Litha* is the time of midsummer, when the sun stops moving north and retires. The sunset was observed and on Midsummer Day the sunset was farthest to the north. At this moment, the sun began to retire. *Litha* probably means something like "retirement". The month following *Litha* was called *Aefterlitha*. In years with three *Litha* months, the first was called Aerlitha (before Litha).

At midwinter, there was two *Giuli* months. *Giuli* has the same root as "Yule" and "wheel". December was *Aergiuli* and January was *Aeftergiuli*. In the moon calendar *Modranecht,* the night before December 25 was the first night without a visible moon in the darkest month. This night was the mother of all coming nights with growing light. Ing/Frey, the god of growing, was reborn and worshipped at the midwinter festival. The boar was a symbol of Ing. Several accounts mention that a hog or boar was sacrificed at the heathen Yule-time. Eating pork is a common Christmas tradition even today.

To return to the marks on the long horn. Most years have twelve new moons and consequently 24 moon phases. Every third year, there is an extra month. It appears that if there were an extra thirteenth month, it would have the same name as the twelfth month. Thus, the angle marks in multiples of 24 can be interpreted as marks of the moon phases. Most years would have 24 phases, but even the years with thirteen months could have 24 marks.

The real purpose of the marks is unknown, but the mark was probably ritually related to the festival of the moon. If we accept that 24 marks indicate an entire year, then the 18 marks of ring 3 below indicate part of a year. On 16 April 413, there was a total solar eclipse in southern Jutland. This happened in the end of the 18th moon phase of the year. The last 18th horizontal angle could mark the eclipse. The rest of the phase marks in this year seem to be placed in ring 5.

Fig 79. Drawing of the 18 sun marks of ring 3 on the long horn

For the Germanics, the moon determined the time of the year, and the sun determined the time of day. The orbit of the sun during night and day was divided in eight eikts. The first three of them, beginning in the northwest, was the night and the last five were the day. Each eikt is symbolised by three universal forces as in the *Ægishjalmr* (figure 68).

Figure 79 is Sorterup's drawing of the 18 marks of ring 3 above. The marks can be called sun marks as they have two concentric rings and eight points like the sun marks of the short horn. Furthermore, they are in six groups of three, probably indicating six eikts. What happened after the six eikts had passed? The total solar eclipse in south Jutland happened at 14.16 local time and the total darkness lasted less than seven minutes. This time was during the seventh eikt: 13.30-16.30. Recording the sun stopped at ring 3 and continued at ring 5 just as the phase marks did. Ring 5 has four sun marks placed in a straight line. They consist of three concentric rings, a stamp that calendar printers used to symbolise the sun. Perhaps the four sun marks could be interpreted as the last two eikts of the day of the eclipse. The two eikts should have three sun marks each but they are both missing one, maybe because the sun is weakened.

The Myth of the Divine Twins

The idea of the Divine Twins is widespread and documented by archaeological finds. The most ancient delineations were two oppositely placed animals of the same species. Depictions of the Divine Twins are seen as early as in the first Neolithic societies. One example of which is from Catalhöyük in modern-day Turkey. Here, a Neolithic settlement (7500-5700 BC) subsisting on agriculture, pottery, the domestication of sheep and cattle, hunting and gathering, existed. Excavations indicate there were no social classes and men and women had the same social status. Many mythical paintings and idols were found. One of the most famous is shown in figure 80: the seated woman of Catalhöyük or the goddess of delivery on a throne. Between her legs is the head of a baby being born. Instead of her head is a hole, so we cannot be sure she had a head. The goddess holds her hands on the heads of two leopards,

80. Idol of burned clay from Catalhöyük in Turkey

two mythical, guiding animals, which may represent the Divine Twins.

The scene may be compared to the delivery goddess of the Gotland stone (figure 52). Probably the most common of all prehistoric picture symbols is a delineation of the Divine Twins. Unfortunately, no systematic study of the meaning of these symbols has yet been made. However, one of the most thorough investigations of the myth was made by Donald Ward (1968). He focused on the Germanic tradition, but he does not include the picture symbols.

Like other deities, the Divine Twins are normally invisible. They can reside in any form they choose and can be present in several places at once. The representation of the Divine Twins varies very much depending on the time, the local cultural tradition and the single artist. The Twins may be opposite pairs of lions, dogs, bears, snakes, dragons, monsters, swans, horses, dolphins, fish, humans, pillars, vases, torches, stars and so on. These representations may correspond to local myths and names that we do not know. In principle, they all represent the two universal forces that guide man, the giving and receiving forces. The third universal force is very often seen between the other two. It could be a delivery goddess, a swan, a human, a face, a tree of life, a sun disk, a ship and so on. In principle, this force is the will or dedication to live.

Many myths of the Divine Twins are known around the world. For example, we have a myth of creation in a liturgical text from Ugarit in Syria (1300 BC). At a time when there was no earth, the father in heaven and the mother in the waters had two sons called Shachar ("activity") and Shalim ("peace"). They created the earth and all the plants and living creatures and they continued to create new living creatures. Even though the myths and the names of the twins depend on the cultural tradition, there are common elements.

Similarly, many Native American creation myths have been studied and almost all of them have Divine Twins as creators. The Fuegian tribe, Yaghan, had a tradition of two divine brothers, who told people how to live. The older brother was lazy and wanted life to be easy for men, and people to be immortal. The active and short-sighted younger brother felt that man must exert himself in order to appreciate what he has. The brothers had an older sister to help them. In some versions of the myth, she was their mother or wife.

In view of the very few written sources of the Germanic Divine Twins, we can look to the available information from three other Indo-European traditions: old Indian Sanskrit literature, Classic Greek literature and old Latvian folk-songs. According to Ward (1968), these three traditions have much in common.

The Indian *Vedas* tell us that the Sky-God had two sons called *Asvins* ("horses"). The Asvins drew a carriage around the earth in one day. In the carriage was their sister, who was called Sureia ("Sun") and Usas ("morning light"). The Sanskrit goddess Usas corresponds to the Latvian goddess *Austra* ("light rising up") and the Germanic goddess *Eostur*. In a Latvian poem, two lights burn on the sea. They are lit by god's sons, who are waiting for the sun-maiden. In Greek tradition, the *Dios Kouroi* ("god's sons") was called Castor ("brilliant") and Polydeukes ("many helps"). The daughter was Helena ("from the sun"). They hatched from an egg as their mother, Leda, and their father, Zeus, were swans. Castor and Polydeukes rescued their sister Helena. The Twins were her brothers but also her husbands, because there were no other gods with which to mate. Castor died every evening and was born again every morning. The Twins never parted and Polydeukes, who was immortal, followed his brother through the world of the dead.

In all three traditions, the Divine Twins helped and guided the rising sun. A similar Germanic myth is probably what is being seen on some Germanic finds, such as the strap ends in figure 33. She was the life source of living creatures. The Twins had many different forms and roles: horses, horse riders, swans, saviours at sea, astral bodies, magic healers, sometimes protectors in battle, sometimes giving fertility to men and women, dancers, protectors of oath and so on.

Germanic Gods

When looking at Germanic religion, Tacitus again provides insight:

> In their ancient songs, their only way of remembering or recording the past they celebrate an earth-born god Tuisto, and his son Mannus, as the origin of their race, as their founders. To Mannus they assign three sons, from whose names, they say, the coast tribes are called Ingaevones; those of the interior, Herminones; all the rest, Istaevones. Some, with the freedom of conjecture permitted by antiquity, assert that the god had several descendants, and the nation several appellations.

Tuisto means "twisted of two" and comes from the earth. Tuisto is probably the double snake described in the section on the meaning of the long horn. *Mannus* means "the creator". Unknown here is whether the Divine Twins had a father, Mannus is a good deduction. However, this passage is mentioned in an Old Icelandic oath: "so help me Frey and Njord and the Omnipotent God".

This heathen omnipotent god is most likely the father and creator called *Mannus* in Latin. The Germanics probably had other names for the Creator and most likely his name was *Tiw*, often represented as a bull, for instance, on top of the sceptre from the Sutton Hoo ship grave (figure 59).

The three sons are the main Germanic gods and their names are obvious. They were worshipped by all Germanic tribes and are eponymous for some tribes. Ingaevones points to the god Ing ("growing"). He was the onrushing Divine Twin and very popular in southern Scandinavia and in pre-Christian England. Later, he received the name *Frey* ("the Lord"). Ing appears in the set of verses in the Anglo-Saxon Rune poem composed in the ninth century.

Ing wæs ærest mid Est-Denum	Ing was first with the East-Danes.
Gesewen secgum, oth he siddan est	Seen they say here later.
Ofer wæg gewat; wæn æfter ran;	Raised above the see, followed the beauty.
Thus heardingas thone hæle nemdun	Thus, the heathens named this hero.

In the poem, the East-Danes are the Angles, who brought the worship of Ing to England. Ing rose from the sea at sunrise and followed the beautiful sun.

Hermiones points to the god Hermund ("high protector") in Norse Mythology. He gave his name to the tribe of Hermundures who lived in Thüringia around AD 100. Hermund is the helping and receiving Divine Twin. Later, he was given the name Njord ("supporter").

The Germanic myth of creation that Tacitus mentions around AD 100 is precisely illustrated on a few gold bracteates, dating around 400 years later. On the bracteate in figure 81, the earth is depicted as a hill and around it lies a serpent with a bird's head at both ends, which must be Tuisto. A neck with a human head is emerging from the birds' beaks, who has to be Mannus. Out of Mannus' mouth appears the leg of one of the two boars. The boars are identifiable by bristles on their backs and in some cases by their long teeth. In southern Sweden, it is normal for the Divine Twins to be represented by boars both on gold bracteates and on helmets. On the bracteate we see both Divine Twins making their daily round of the earth.

Tacitus' information on the third sun of Mannus is not completely correct, for this son has to be a daughter. Istaevones points to the

Fig 81. Gold bracteate from Holmetorp, Öland, around AD 500 (Hauck cat. 279).

goddess Eostur, also called Ostara, Austria and so on. She is the sister to the Divine Twins, who brings forth the sun and all living creatures. In Latvian songs, the goddess associated with the Divine Twins was called Austra ("light rising up").

According to Bede, the heathen Angles in England had a month *Eostur* (April), that was named after their goddess Eostur. They made sacrifices to her during this month. The Christian Easter was named after the heathen festival. A goddess with a similar name was worshipped in practically all Indo-European cultures. Estonians and Austrians were named after this goddess. In ancient Egypt, her name was Aset, but the Greeks called her Isis. In figure 33, we see Austra rising from the horizon, guided by the Divine Twins, depicted here as sea lions. The symbol illustrates the words about Ing in the rune poem: Raised above the sea, followed the beauty.

Tacitus provides more information about the Germanic Divine Twins:

> Amongst the Naharvalians is shown a grove, sacred to devotion extremely ancient. Over it a Priest presides

apparelled like a woman; but according to the explication of the Romans, it is Castor and Pollux who are here worshipped. This Divinity is named *Alcis*. There are indeed no images here, no traces of an extraneous superstition: yet their devotion is addressed to young men and to brothers.

The Latin word *Alcis* is the name of the pair of gods, most probably the Divine Twins. The Germanic word could be *Alchi* and has the same root as the Gothic words *alh* ("protector") and *alhs* ("temple or protection"). The Indo-European *alek* means "protection, help". The Germanic name of the pair of twins emerges in the rune name *alchi* (figure 74). The name *Alchi* also turned up in a remarkable Germanic inscription clearly related to the worship of the Divine Twins. The inscription is found on the cups shown in figure 82.

The two cups belong to a rich grave in a burial mound from AD 275 in Himlingøje, in Zealand. The cups are made of silver. Each cup has a gilded frieze along the edge. The figures on the friezes are stamped, and some of them are identical. Their irregular sequence points to a cryptic inscription similar to the inscription on the long

Fig 82. Silver cups from Himlingøje, Zealand, around AD 275

Fig 83. Figures from the Himlingøje Cups

horn. It can be deciphered and translated (Rasmussen 2004):

Frieze 1:   Alchi reichi alricher   meaning: "Alchi powers reach everywhere"

Frieze 2:   Alchi reia Alchi reia   meaning: "Alchi be praised, Alchi be praised"

Fig 84. Wooden idol found in a well at Oss-Ussen, the Netherlands, height 75 cm (Silkeborg 2001)

The text is obviously part of the ritual worshipping of the Divine Twins. Drinking from the cups was probably similar to drinking from a pair of horns. The silver cups and the Golden Horns are ritual objects. Their cryptic inscriptions are exceptional, because they are the only old Germanic inscriptions of some length and because they give us valuable insight into the Germanic religion.

One of the figures on the friezes features two heads, one on top of the other (figure 83). The lower head is upside down – a common symbol for the Divine Twins, found on several Germanic drinking horn mountings. This head-to-head symbol is found in Nordic Bronze Age carvings. The head-to-head symbol is also found as a wooden carving from the Germanic time. Very few wooden idols have been found. They are mostly found in moors, such as that in figure 84, which shows an idol from Oss-Ussen, the Netherlands, 200 BC. We see two human figures feet-to-feet. Arms and legs are marked and the upper one seems to have horns. It is most likely a depiction of the Divine Twins.

Germanic gods of prosperity

The short horn (figures 2 and 57) suggests that the Divine Twins were gods of prosperity, evident in their attributes on the uppermost ring of heaven and the second ring of the worker. Here, we find farming and lunar symbols. Other finds that testify to the twins being gods of prosperity are the gold bracteates. Funen was a Germanic religious centre for a long period. The procession of Mother Earth, as described by Tacitus, occurred on an *island in the ocean* – in all probability, Funen. Paraphernalia associated with such processions has been found on Funen, dating to as late as the tenth century. The period of the great migrations (AD 375-575) is also a period of great gold finds in Denmark. The area around the village Gudme ("god's home"), on Funen, was the royal seat of a leading Danish king, where exceptional, rich gold artefacts have been found,

Fig 85. Gold bracteate from Gudme, Funen, around AD 500 (Hauck cat. 51,3)

including some of the most elaborate gold bracteates with runic inscriptions.

The photographic reproduction of the bracteate in figure 85 has an extra frame. For now, it is the inner illustration that concerns us. The scene can be interpreted as a representation of the Greek version of the myth of the Divine Twins. In the middle is Castor (Ing), always accompanied by his twin brother Polydeukes (Njord). They pass through the Realm of Death and meet their sister Helena (Eostur), who gives new life to Castor.

Ing dies every night, but he is brave and dances. He holds the key to his new life in one hand. In the other, he has a gold coin or a gold bracteate. A line from his head points to his immortal brother, Njord, probably to indicate that it is his brother who leads. Njord has a pointer to show the way and a gold coin. The lizard informs the viewer that the scene is taking place in the Underworld.

The twins meet the giver of birth and morning light, Eostur, who helps them cross to a new life. She touches Ing with a ring, the symbol of regeneration. The ring features a three-pointed star, the symbol of growing life. Around her neck is a tree of life. She has wings and a skirt. She brings forth all living beings – even celestial bodies. Indeed, she is often depicted as standing on celestial bodies on the bracteates.

Above the Divine Twins, an eagle is following their journey. The mythical eagle is the heavenly goddess, who brings the souls of the deceased to the realm of death and is connected with the warrior elite (see the chapter on Sutton Hoo). The goddess' name *Hreth* means "the Horrible" or even "the old Hag". Some Gothic and Saxon chieftains assumed the eagle symbol from the Sarmatians around AD 300, and the powerful Danish kings on Funen seem to have adopted it, in their own version, in the AD 400s. Despite being a god, Ing, a mortal, needed his heavenly mother to take care of his immortal soul. Thus, the eagle brings his soul to where regeneration occurs (for more see sections on Sutton Hoo and the Franks casket).

The runic inscription is UNDR. In Danish, we have almost the same word *under*, meaning "wonder" in English. This makes a lot of sense. Rebirth is certainly a wonder. A person carrying such an amulet would have believed in the rebirth of Ing, and in their own rebirth. A regenerative religion is typical among ancient agricultural societies.

Of the gold bracteates, the most common type (type C) features a male head on top of a mythical horse, such as that illustrated in figure 86. Another gold bracteate (Hauck cat. 147), in the same style as that in figure 86, was found with coins in a hoard dating to around AD 480. The two bracteates must have been produced by the same smith. Bracteates with plaited hairstyles as shown in figure

Fig 86. Gold bracteate from Funen, AD 480s (Hauck cat. 58)

86 are rare: five from eastern Funen, three from eastern Zealand, two near Kiel and three from Sweden and Norway combined (Axboe 2007) – perhaps indicative of where the Danes from Funen held power.

The bracteate in figure 86 has three runic inscriptions:

HOUAR	meaning	*The Raiser*
ALU	meaning	*I bring growth*
LAThU AADUAALLIIA	meaning	*I invoke growing*

HOUAR, ending in R, must be substantive. It is related to "high". "The Raiser" must be the name of the horse. On the C bracteate, the horse runs beside the god Ing/Frey. In Norse Mythology, transcribed around AD 1200, we have reminiscences of old Germanic religious ideas:

"Skinfaxe with the sparkling mane that shines over air and earth is Day's horse".
Day must be another name for Ing. Skinfaxe must be another name for Houar. The mythical horse that whirls around actually represents the daily movement of the sky. It turns the firmament during the day, bringing with it daylight. The legs have fins because the horse runs across the sky. The horns of the horse symbolise the power of procreation. The scene on the bracteate is the everyday movement of heaven. And note the inclusion of the motherly eagle again.

ALU is the most common inscription on gold bracteates. The word is related to the Latin *alere* ("nourish") and the Germanic *al* ("grow"). The suffix *-U* is used in the present tense, first person singular. The expression "I bring growth" comes from the god Ing. He runs beside the horse and takes part in turning the firmament. Ing is young and strong as evident in his magnificent shining hair. He is the giving, active and brave twin, which we find on the left side of the uppermost ring on the short horn in figure 57. He follows the sun as it rises in the morning and sets at the sunset. The bracteate itself expresses "I bring growth".

The ALU runic inscription is also found on an urn from the Spong Hill cemetery in Norfolk, suggesting the meaning could be the imperative: "Grow!"

LAThU AADUAALLIIA with the –*U* suffix on *LAThU* is the first person singular and means "I invite". The runes of *AADUAALLIIA* are doubled in this inscription; something not seen anywhere else. Removing the doubled runes leaves the word *ADUALIA,* which is related to the Latin *adolescere* ("to grow up") and *adultus* ("to become adult"). Thus, the inscription could mean "I invoke growing". That which is "growing" rapidly is produced by Ing. The double runes may have been used for artistic reasons; to depict "growing", the individual runic characters grow themselves.

The worship of the Germanic Divine Twins is demonstrated by a

Fig 86b. Remains of the Uppåkra Temple

Fig 87. Metal beaker with seven gold bands, AD 500s, found in Uppåkra

precious find at Uppåkra in Scania, excavated 2000-2004. Uppåkra was a central religious centre during the Germanic and Viking Ages. The metal beaker in figure 87 was found in the temple of Uppåkra. A unique glass bowl was found alongside the metal beaker. The beaker and bowl had been deposited under the clay floor of the temple in the AD 500s. The beaker is 17 cm high and divided into seven rings just like the Golden Horns (Larsson 2002). The gold foil ornaments are impressed in the same form. There are only two different ornaments on the gold bands and one of them is shown in figure 87.

The Uppåkra Temple was a building situated in front of a great hall. The post-holes from the four pillars are four metres deep (figure 86b). These pillars could not have supported an ordinary roof; more likely a very tall open shed. The wooden walls were probably the enclosure of the temple. The fireplace was probably used for sacrificing animals. A similar temple, also situated in front of a great hall, was found at Lejre (The Land of Legends) on Zealand. The buildings in Lejre date from the AD 500s and were probably the residence of Hrotulf/Rolf Krake. In Gudme, on Funen, a similar pair of buildings was found from the AD 400s. These buildings may have belonged to the Danish King Scyld or his successors. *Beowulf* lines 175-179 read:
Sometimes they pledged at holy temples
Sacred honouring, in words bid
That them the demon-slayer would offer help
From the pain of the people such was their habits
The hope of heathens.

The ornament in figure 88 consists of two entwined humans and horses. The close connection and the opposite position of the two humans tell us that these are the Divine Twins. Their magnificent hairstyles indicate their heavenly status. The humans seem to be holding onto a horse leg. The leg has three fingers, which may

Fig 88. Decoration on the gold bands of the metal beaker in figure 87

Fig 89. Bracteate from Zealand (Hauck cat. 105)

represent a bird claw. The humans and the horses symbolise invisible spiritual powers. Only characteristic parts of their bodies need to be shown. One of the pair is likely Frey and Skinfaxe, with Frey residing in Skinfaxe and leading him; two aspects of the same creature.

Most of the gold bracteates wish for good harvest and prosperity.

Another example of a gold bracteate from Zealand features only one human creature, figure 89.

The runic inscription reads

SALUS ALU   meaning   *I let prosperity prevail*

The word *SALUS* was inscribed on several Roman medals. It means "health" and "prosperity". *ALU* means "I bring growth". The depicted god is one of the Divine Twins, the gods of prosperity. Perhaps both of the Divine Twins are depicted, one of them as a wolf. The fore part of the animal's body is strongly built and makes it unlikely to be a dog. Several bracteates have been found with a heavenly wolf instead of a heavenly horse. Wolf bracteates are found in the area of the eastern Danes. Hrothulf/Rolf Krake succeeded and probably killed Hrothgar as the superior Danish king around AD 525. This bracteate was found in Zealand at Hrothulf's royalseat at Lejre. He was also a Wulfing. Another difference between the bracteate types in figure 85 and 89 is that the bird in figure 89 is not an eagle but more likely a raven, though still mistress of the other world – "the old Hag" – and as usual she whispers to Ing/Frey. Hrothulf's surname was *Krake,* which meant "raven" and he probably had a raven standard. The raven standard was used by Danish kings for the next 500 years. The Swastika is a symbol of Heaven, indicating that the creatures on the bracteate are invisible and spiritual. The eight balls may represent the eight directions of heaven.

Frey and Njord

Around AD 1220, the Christian Icelandic writer Snorre Sturluson gave a thorough description of Norse Mythology as a delusion. He writes:

> Njord dwells in Noatun, which is in heaven. He rules the course of the wind and checks the fury of the sea and of fire. He is invoked by seafarers and by fishermen. He is so rich and wealthy that he can give broad lands and abundance to those who call on him for them. He was fostered in Vanaheim, but the Vanir gave him as a hostage to the gods. Njord has at his disposal countless of alters and temples.
>
> Njord begot two children: a son, by name Frey, and a daughter, by name Freya. They were fair of face, and mighty. Frey is the most famous of the Aesir. He rules over rain and sunshine, and over the fruits of the earth.

This description of the roles of Njord and Frey fits very well with the roles ascribed to the Germanic Divine Twins. Many legends of Norse Mythology confirm that Njord and Frey developed from the Divine Twins. Snorre himself says that Frey is another name for Ing.

Frey, Freya and Njord were ancient gods and, in the original myth, they were born at the same time. Snorre was Christian, so the idea of the daily regeneration of Frey was difficult for him to comprehend. Perhaps that is why the myth changed, with Njord taking on the role of father because he was the immortal twin. There is no issue with Njord being a father as a god can be both father and brother. Freya was a daughter, but as a goddess she was able to be daughter, sister, mistress and mother to the twins.

Around AD 100, Tacitus mentioned the gods Ing and Hermund and, a thousand years later, these gods were still a living tradition although they had new names. The Germanics did not transcribe their religious myths, but depended on oral tradition. Furthermore, Germanic ethnic groups were rather independent of each other. Given these circumstances, it is remarkable that the idea of the Divine Twins was so widespread and only changed little and slowly.

The name Frey, for instance, is related to the Indo-European *pro-* meaning "forward, forth". The Danish words *fro* and *frejdig* mean "advancing". The Old Norse *frjo* means "seed, offspring". Frey was the growing, advancing twin. Some scholars believe that Frey means "Lord". It is possible that the meaning Lord emerged because there was a god with the name Frey and he was the lord.

A few gold bracteates have runic inscriptions. The gold bracteate from Darum (figure 90) seems to have the name of the depicted god. The runic inscription is

FRØHILA LAThU   which translates as   *Holy Frey I invoke*

FRØ means "seed", a common name for the growing god Frey. The first three runes could also be transcribed as *FRO*, perhaps relating to words such as the Danish *fro.* It is a good name for Frey. *HILA* means "holy". *LAThU* with an *–U* suffix is the first person singular and means "I invite!". The amulet invokes Frey to help the carrier of the bracteate.

Danish kings divided their territory into nearly one hundred districts, each called a *herred* in order to control the mobilisation of the armed men. This practice started around AD 700 and the names of the *herreds* are very old. Some of the herreds are named after pagan deities, but only Frø's Herred is named after Frey. Frø's Herred is the district where Ribe is located, indicative of a once great sanctuary for Frey close to Darum, near Ribe, where the amulet was found (figure 90). A vast number of place names derived from the name *Frey* indicate that he was the most popular god within Scandinavia

90. Gold bracteate from Darum, near Ribe, in southwest Jutland, around AD 500. (Hauck cat. 42)

before the Viking Age. In England, place names such as *Friston* may pertain to Frey.

The god Ing was also called Fro/Frey around AD 500. There is further evidence of this in *Beowulf*, where we are told that the powerful Danish king, Scyld, was buried by being sent away alone on a ship (Lines 27-29):

Then Scyld departed at the destined time,
Still in his full-strength, to fare in the protection of the Lord Frea
He they carried to the sea's surf.

That the Heatobeardan king Froda was also called Frothi was mentioned in the chapter on Barwith Syssel. His name is related to the god Fro/Frey. Freawaru was going to mary Ingeld, son of Froda.

Her name is related to Frea/Frey and Ingeld is related to Ing. All these examples indicate that the names Ing and Frea/Frey were used in southern Scandinavia around AD 500.

The name Njord is related to the Old Norse *njota* and the Old English *neotan*, both meaning "receive, take, nourish". These words can be traced back to the Indo-European *neud* meaning "acquire, utilise, go fishing". *Nodens* is a similar Celtic deity associated with healing, the sea and hunting.

Tacitus recorded the name *Hermund* ("High protector") for the supporting Divine Twin. In Norse Mythology, it is the god Hermod, who guides dead souls through the Underworld. He may be related to Hermund or the Greek god Hermes. The personal name *Herman* was used by the southern Germanics and it may have related to Hermund. The existence of place names Hermund is currently uncertain, but there are plenty of place names in Scandinavia related to Njord.

Njord place names are predominantly waterways such as rivers and inlets. In Denmark, we find Nors Sø, Norå, Nærå, Nærum. In Sweden, Njärdhavi, Närtuna. In Iceland, Njardvik. Western Norway has many fjords and sounds, many of which are named after Njord. For instance, Nærøy and Nidaros (now Trondheim) and four fjords called Njardvik. Near Ålesund is the farm Njardarland with an area called Noatun ("Njord's court") and a moor with three ships graves.

Indeed, the common ship graves in Scandinavia deserve to be addressed as do the stone ship settings. The ship grave enabled the invisible dead soul to sail with the invisible ship around the earth. Bronze Age rock carvings show that the Divine Twins took part in that journey. Indeed, it is probable that the ship grave tradition was bound to the ship of the Divine Twins, which is the ship of Njord, the saving god.

Njord, the god of ships and fishing, was very popular in western Norway from Roman times until Christian times. Around AD 1800, an old married couple from the Hardanger area went fishing in a boat. One night, they caught fish for an entire week and the woman exclaimed: "Thank you he shall have, Njor, for this time".

What about the origin of *Norway*? The earliest written version is *Nortuagia* from AD 840 at the monastery of Durham, northern England. Then around AD 890, when Ottar sailed from Hålogaland in the northern part of present-day Norway to England, his report was recorded at the English court. He went south and, on his left, he passed *Nordweg*. Many scholars think this name means "the way to North"; thus, it is unlikely that Ottar, who was going south, would have used this expression. It is highly unlikely that a country would be named after the direction to somewhere else. It is more probable that the meaning of the name was "Njord's ways"; the fjords and sounds in present-day western Norway. Ottar also used the name "Nordmanna land", which is normally translated as "Men from the North". Indeed, I believe the *Nor*mans originally meant people for whom Njord was an important god. The Norwegians are called *Nordmænd* in Danish.

The traditional gods in Scandinavia, those before the Aesir, were called the Vanir ("fair"). We know them as Njord, Frey and Freya. The introduction of the new Aesir religion met with some difficulties. The Viking Period in Scandinavia was a long religious fight between the goddess Freya and the new god Odin. Freya was originally the mistress of the Other World but Odin gradually assumed that role. He used Freya's throne, her eagle mantle, her Brisingamen necklace, the drink of immortality and the runes as is described in the Old Norse *Völuspa* poem. The war between the Aesir and Vanir began when the Aesir stole a decorated gold idol of Freya and burned it in

Odin's hall. This occurred three times. But the women were upset that they could not worship Freya. Vanir were not allowed in the halls of the Aesir. But then the women started to worship Odin's wife as if she were Freya. Then the Aesir accepted that the Vanir could live in Asgard and be worshipped alongside Odin.

It is quite clear from this account that the Aesir religion was introduced by military force. In fact, it was not spread among all chieftains and not used by the lower classes. Viking society, with its centralised power, was in many ways different from tribal society. The production and use of the valuable Viking ships caused a new division of the country into adequate districts. Built-up areas appeared along the coast, because the king guaranteed their security. A new runic alphabet, with only 16 runes, and independent of the old religion, emerged around AD 700. In Scandinavia, the first powerful worshipper of Odin was the king of Scania, Ivar Vidfadme. He died around AD 705.

Odin, the heavenly master, was original a forefather spirit (Rasmussen 2006). According to Norse mythology, he stole the drink of immortality from the earth goddess. With this drink, he secured eternal life in heaven for his dead worshippers. At Uppåkra, in Scania, was a major centre for worship of Odin. The king and the warriors dedicated their life to Odin as well as the lives of the men they killed. In return, they had Odin's protection in battle and immortal life together with Odin in heaven (Valhalla). In the AD 900s, the Danish king controlled the country for the first time and his power and wealth increased considerably. In this period, of the last heathen king in Denmark, the Aesir religion flourished. There were sacrifices of animals and humans. Most of the amulets from this century were formed as Thor's hammers.

From Old Norse literature, it is clear that Frey and Njord were still worshipped by some local chieftains during the Viking Age. For example, in Egil Skallagrimsson's Saga. Egil Skallagrimsson was a great Viking warrior and skald. His father, Skallagrim, was a rich independent farmer in Norway. Around AD 900, the Christian Norwegian king, Harold Fair-hair, brutally suppressed the independent farmers and many of them migrated to Iceland so as to keep their freedom. This migration is comparable to the migration of the Angles from Jutland. In both cases, the purpose was to maintain freedom and to have land that was not occupied.

In AD 930, when Harold was 80 years old he left his kingship to his son Eric Blood-axe. He was even more brutal. Egil Skallagrimsson travelled from Iceland to Norway in order to claim his inheritance at the Thing, but he was attacked by Erik Blood-axe's men and outlawed. In a poem Egil said:

Protective deity of the land,
Make the tyrant flee;
May Freyr and Njordr hate the
Oppressor of his people, he who has
Violated the sanctuary.

In Iceland, a similar oath was common.
So help me Frey and Njord and the Omnipotent God.

Speculations have been made as to the identity of the "Omnipotent God". Odin can be eliminated, because Odin was not worshipped in Iceland, which had no king. The Omnipotent God was probably Mannus (examined earlier), the creator of the world, father of the twins Frey and Njord. The Germanic creator-god also went by the names Tiw, Tyr and Ti. He was represented as a bull or a stag (figures 57, 58, 59 and 60).

The Origin of Religion

The goddess of birth and the Divine Twins were central religious figures for all Germanic tribes. Where did these ideas come from? Pictures and idols tell us that the ideas were present at a very early stage (at least 7500 BC) and spread all over the world. The myth, the picture symbols and the names of the deities depend on local traditions, but the general idea has been preserved through the ages. This preservation was only possible because the ideas corresponded to people's experiences. Lasting religious ideas have to be based on the most fundamental experiences of human life.

Religious ideas reflect humanity's attitude to life. Other ideas may give the individual advice on how to act in various situations, but religious ideas offer advice for every situation in life. Most important in life are the phenomena inside the individual and interactions with other people. Religion provides answers in these matters. The Latin *religio* is composed of *re* ("again, repeat") and *ligare* ("to bind, fasten"). Myths provides models for the behaviour of the individual.

The basic experiences are had in the first three years of life. During this time, the human soul is formed inside through outside stimuli and interactions. We do not remember how our psyche was formed. The experiences of early childhood are preserved in the unconscious mind. The stimuli of early childhood are very much the same for all children and have not changed much since antiquity. We start out as a helpless creature, who has to be picked up and carried by a gracious mother.

Blood samples show that a baby and mother produce a hormone (oxytocin) when they share bodily contact – even when sharing only eye contact. Experiments involving adults inhaling this hormone prove that it reduces anxiety and distrust in others. Babies will die if they do not have human contact, and despite having their physical needs met. A baby needs engagement, contact and experiences. The little child learns body language and spoken language as they seek human contact and, consequently, needs to communicate. Once interaction satisfies these needs, the baby has a happy feeling of being together and co-operating. Normally, a baby is friendly and enjoys stimulating contact, and develops a basic trust in life and in other people.

The first happy experience of interaction babies have is preserved unconsciously as a happy state of mind, which can be called "basic trust". Over the course of their life, this happy feeling is reinforced countless times – probably evoked by hormones. In fact, we have a need for interaction the rest of our lives and we try to fulfil that need in many ways. If we are left to ourselves with our problems, we worry about our private condition. But, in a friendly community, we feel safe and do not worry too much. Most human activities are social. Anything we do will have relation to other people.

The oldest and most common religious idea we know of is the mother of life, the goddess of birth and death. The idea of a deity, who accepts and supports anybody is based on the first experiences in human life. Babies do not know how helpless they are. They probably experience that everything comes by itself. They have a feeling of vitality, omnipotence and unity. An older child, or an adult person, who has a similar experience of vitality may describe it as joy, strength, will-power, wisdom, peace, love or compassion. Normally, we cannot control these feelings as they are mainly caused by unconscious processes. However, religious rituals may invoke such feelings.

Rituals involving the participation of several people from the community impact strongly on an individual's state of mind due to the unconscious body language of such rituals. Participants of a ritual involving eating, drinking, singing, dancing or sacrifices are able to feel power or truth inside. The unconscious influence comes from the body language, consumption or voices within and of the company. The effect on the mind is similar to the baby's experience of a mother taking care of them and unconsciously evoke the feeling of vitality from early childhood. The individual will feel a capacity of life inside, and forget their own problems. They will feel helped by some invisible force described as the spirit of the deity. Indeed, the deity is present inside the performers during the ritual as a collective spiritual experience. Faithful individuals can maintain the feeling of strength and courage for a longer time after the ritual, but it helps to repeat the ritual regularly. The experience of faith in god may be described as being like a child again, as putting your destiny into god's hands, as delighting in the beauty of life or as being grateful to the creator of life.

The myths about the mother of life developed as social creations when the members of the community took part in the rituals of that community and spoke of their experiences of the rituals. Idols or paintings of the deity are also a kind of myth. Despite being created by an individual, they express a common experience. The Mother of Life was the symbol of unity for the ethnic group. She ensured the survival and flourishing of the community.

The mother of life was not the biological mother of any specific individual; she was a myth told in the society, giving life and death to all individuals and even to all animals and plants. She accepts any kind of life and any kind of behaviour or destiny of the living creatures. The myth of the mother of life makes the believers understand how all life comes forth and disappears. She makes dead organisms disappear in the earth and living ones come out of the earth. She is also the one who can bestow new life on deceased human beings.

The goddess can be seen in imaginations, but she is normally invisible. The popular goddess had many names and many myths. In farming societies, a common name was Mother Earth. The idols had many forms: a she-goat, a frog, a living tree, a pole, a female. The goddess was sometimes represented by a face as in figure 36b or just eyes, such as in figure 24. The observer might have the feeling of a baby watching their mother's face.

From interaction with members of the community, the child develops physical and psychic abilities. One side of interaction is observation, understanding, nourishment and compassion. This ability can be called the receiving force and it develops from birth. On the other side of the interaction is the moving and speaking of the child themselves, which begins after about a year. As early as six months old, the human child develops a feeling of having their own will and they recognise that they are interacting with another person. The ability to act can be called the giving force. The two forces became part of our minds when we were babies and drive our minds unconsciously our whole lives through. Human life is guided by the giving force and the receiving force and these universal forces are represented by the different characters of the Divine Twins. The presence of two forces of the mind might be one reason for the widespread belief in the Divine Twins.

There are different myths about twins or brothers from many tribes. They are called deities or heroes, but the brothers always seem to have different characters. Different aspects of the Divine Twins were identified with by different people, depending on the role or the project of the people. Believers may have felt that one or both of the

Divine Twins helped them. The intent to be creative and active may have been understood as the presence of the giving Twin. The intent to accept and enjoy may have been understood as the presence of the receiving Twin.

We have knowledge of some rituals for the Divine Twins: dancing, singing, libation, the sacrifice of animals and humans and, primarily, the drinking ritual of the Germanic tribes. Like all rituals, the effect would be the participants feeling the presence of the spiritual force. Imagining the Divine Twins at the rituals probably revived the two forces from childhood.

According to most of the myths and delineations, the Divine Twins are always the same species, sex and age and they always stay together. Indeed, the Divine Twins are a very strong symbol of being together, solidarity and co-operation. Even today we light two candles in order to create an atmosphere of being together. In Chinese Taoism, people who want a companion are advised to put things, which are two of a kind, in many places in their home. According to the myths and legends, the function of the Divine Twins was to guide the sun and human beings through life and the afterlife.

The Divine Twins are symbols of friendly human community. They are models for tribal society. They help each other and they help believers. They are equal partners, who accept each other even if they have very different characters and roles. The idea of the Divine Twins belongs to tribal society, to which they are perfectly suited deities. Being twins, their ethnic relation could not be closer. The individuals in the tribe take care of each other and they only have the tribe for help and protection.

The Divine Twins are models of brotherhood and fellowship. The motto of the French Revolution was "liberty, equality, fraternity", but the third one seems to have been forgotten today. Brotherhood means helping your brother and receiving help without conditions. Brotherhood was essential to the tribal community.

Palaeolithic hunters lived in small ethnic groups and some made many cave paintings: undoubtedly, some of the painted animals were meant to be helpful spirits, but there are hardly any examples of pairs of twins. Only some aboriginal Australian groups have rock paintings and myths of a pair of brothers. One example is a pair who were born from the earth as dingoes and then created all living creatures. Later they were humans and now they are snakes and create rain and storm.

Why did the Divine Twins not emerge before the farmers? The answer may be that agriculture and the domestication of animals demand planning. Harvest and slaughtering must be planned far in advance and here the receiving older twin was most helpful. For sowing and growing, the young twin is most helpful (see the chapter on Germanic gods of prosperity). In the farming community, there has to be room for people with different abilities and the individual may have to change their role, according to the circumstances in their lives.

The Divine Twins were gods of prosperity and guided the human activities of the Germanic farmers. The rituals and festivals were connected to the seasons of the year, such as sowing, harvesting and the yule time sacrifice of a boar. The whole community or, at least, the local settlement took part in the rituals, whereby the unconscious body language of those present expressed the inner feeling of being led by the gods. The individual conviction that the gods took care of the community was essential motivation for the activities of the individuals.

The Germanic ethnic groups farmed together but the men also fought together. Men from the community partook in the drinking ritual with the two horns or cups. The body language here, the ovations and the consumption gave the individual an inner feeling of the presence of the Divine Twins. The ritual reinforced the commitment of the group. The individual's conviction of the presence of the gods in the fellow tribe members made it easier for the individual to accept decisions regarding war or migration. These rituals ensured a strong following for the tribe's chieftain.

As early as around AD 200 a new faith in the Aesir gods emerged among the East Saxons. Foreigners became chieftains and they worshiped their own ancestor god, Woden. The deceased worshippers would have a splendid life in Heaven with Woden. This saviour religion was only popular among some chieftains and their professional warriors. It was not common in England. Around AD 700, the first Scandinavian king, who worshipped the Aesir gods, is known. This became the religion of the Viking kings and their warrior elite until Christianity was introduced around AD 1000. The ruling class was the first to convert.

Even in tribal society, the individual could have troubles that could not be overcome with the help of their allies. They would feel insecure when they were sick or when they were travelling away from the tribe. It was precisely in these situations that the Divine Twins were called upon for help and advice. Most Germanic tribes had myths in which the Divine Twins were said to be the ancestors of the tribe. These myths were often related to migration of the tribe. They guided voyages; the golden horns were almost certainly sacrificed to the Twins on the occasion of migration.

What happened to the Divine Twins?

The social system changed from tribes to central kingship during the Germanic period. The religious ideas had to be changed, too. When a tribe migrated, warfare was inevitable, so the tribe needed an authoritarian leader. The east Germanic tribes were the first to migrate and some of them, such as the Goths, had powerful kings. Furthermore, people of different tribes were mixed with the migration. The king no longer had common cause with a tribe. A central power needs a central religion. The Roman Emperor Constantine chose Christianity from among several religions as the central religion. Christianity was a religion with strict laws and the Church was a strong centralised, controlled organisation. The Germanic kings who seized power in the former Roman provinces accepted Christianity as the official religion because it was convenient for their administration.

Christianity inculturated much of the older idea of the Divine Twins. The Bible says that god created night and day on the first day. Night and day were twin gods of the Canaanites. Night and day helped god create the rest of the world. On the third day, they created the sun. In the Book of Genesis, two angels visited Lot and helped him. Two angels also visited Abraham and helped him.

Most of the towns in the Greco-Roman world had temples for the Divine Twins, whom they called Castor and Polydeukes among other names. The Christians replaced the heathen twin-gods with a pair of saints. For example, around AD 530 Pope Felix IV changed the dedication of a temple in Rome from the heathen twins of the city to a church for the brothers, St Cosmas and St Damiano. These saints were physicians, one of the functions of the Divine Twins.

91. Sun-relief in the Church of Santa Maria Quintanilla de la Vinas, Burgos around AD 580

All Germanic people worshipped the Divine Twins as evident by the decorations with an opposed pair of animals of the same species. Many such pairs adorned medieval churches. Pairs of angels became very popular among the Christianised Germanics during the Middle Ages. Figure 91 shows an early example, from around AD 580, from northern Spain, where Gothic kings ruled. The Goths here, like most of the Christianised Germanic tribes, were Arian Christians and opposed to the Catholic church. The Arians were the first to use the cross as a Christian symbol. It was an equal armed cross that was attributed the same symbolism as in heathen belief: "the spiritual world". The Arians did not believe in saints but they did believe in angels. Inside the ring in the centre is the inscription SOL meaning sun, and angels are on either side presenting the Sun. The scene probably depicts the creation of the sun. The inscription reads:

(h)OC EXIGVVM EXIGVA OFF(ert) DO(mina) FLAMMOLA VOTUM D(eo)

This small vow/vowed gift the unworthy (exigua) lady Flammola offers to God.

It seems angels assumed the role of the Divine Twins. Angels had a similar function to the twins: both could dwell with humans. Like all spiritual beings, they could be several places at the same time. They could even take reside inside humans. They guided people. Even in our time many people still believe in guiding angels.

The most distinguishing feature of the Germanic view of life was probably the belief in personal freedom. There was a tendency among Germanic families to let the younger generation leave home, which could lead to colonisation and migration – even today. In Protestantism, the individual has a more personal relation to God than in Catholicism. It is probably not a coincidence that the modern spread of Protestantism fits within the Germanic speaking areas. In the Middle Ages, East Anglia was different from the rest of England by having the greatest number of Freemen. This was due to the tradition of the Angles. East Anglia also had most risings against the central Catholic power in London. Martin Luther had great influence here. During the reign of Mary, Queen of Scots, many Protestants were burned at the stake as punishment for their beliefs. 82% of them were from the nine eastern counties out of the 50 counties in England.

In the Viking Age, in Scandinavia, Frey and Njord were worshipped and they had almost the same function as the Divine Twins in the Germanic Age. Christianity was successfully introduced into Scandinavia around AD 1000. The Danish king brought the first bishops from England and established the first Christian town in Denmark near the old Aesir centre of Uppåkra in Scania. This town, Lund, was a copy of London, with both having the same original Latin name: *Londinium/ Londonia*. Christianity was exercised predominantly in the towns during the Catholic period. In private homes, in the countryside, old habits were alive, and people worshipped the old fertility gods, the Vanir. The Vanir survived as Catholic Saints. Freya gained new life as god's mother, the Virgin Mary. Next to the Virgin Mary, the most popular saint was Saint Nicolas, Santa Claus, the patron saint of travellers at sea, of merchants, of harvesters, of the poor and of children. He has much the same function as Njord.

Saint Nicolas was very popular because he could bring prosperity. In Denmark, his popular name was Niels or Nis. It was a common believe that Nis lived in the stable or the attic, ensuring that sickness and failure of crops stayed away. Sacrifices of food had to be made to him especially near Christmas time, probably on Saint Nicolas' day 6th December. This custom can still be found. Nowadays, *nisser* exist as elves at Christmas time and Santa Claus as the bringer of Christmas gifts.

What happened to Frey is more crucial. Jesus Christ seems to have some of the same traits as Frey: a dying and resurrecting god. Also Saint John the Baptist may have some of Frey's functions. At Midsummer, Frey was worshipped with rituals at holy creeks and bonfires. These heathen traditions are still practiced in Denmark on the evening of Saint John's day, the 24th June.

The ritual drinking, similar to that for the Divine Twins, seems to have survived. In the Viking Age, there were drinking parties with toasts to the gods. In the Middle Ages, there were toasts to the saints. Figure 92 is a so-called *ølhøne* ("beer hen") used in the

Fig 92. An ølhøne from western Norway, 1800s

Fig 93. Embroidered towel from northern Zealand

1800s in western Norway. All of the participants drank from it.

The name and form is a very old tradition, possibly going back to the symbols of the Divine Twins. When a toast is proposed for a spiritual being today, it may hark back to the drinking ritual for the Divine Twins.

Contemporary reminiscences of the Divine Twins can be seen in countries where Germanic ethnic groups have settled. The oath "by Gemini" is clearly addressed to the Divine Twins. A pair of horns or antlers is often mounted on walls inside or outside, in particular, above doors. The original meaning was protection from the Divine Twins, but this has long been forgotten (see also the gable decorations in figure 39).

Folk art traditions live on for many generations. Some folklore embroideries feature motives of the mother of life and the Divine Twins. In figure 93, the mother of life is represented by a bird, a heart and a woman, while the Divine Twins are represented by two standing riders, two birds and two plants. Such motives can also be found on paintings or woodcarvings on old furniture and in old houses.

Looking at many contemporary customs, superstitions and celebrations, the firm stamp of those heathen religions can clearly be seen. So much so that we can say that Heathenism is still with us today, and is still being practised, albeit unknown by most of those practicing it.

Figures

1. Reconstruction of the two horns based on drawings.

2. The uppermost ring of the short horn; Drawing by Paulli.

3. Silver mounting of one of the two drinking horns from Taplow in Berkshire.

4. Replica of the helmet from the Sutton Hoo ship burial.

5. Wall painting from Pompeii.

6. The Germanic runic alphabet in the outer circle and the sound of the runes in the inner circle.

7. Three syssels in southern Jutland that were once the homeland of the Angles.

8. Finds from the first half of the AD 400s (Böhme 1986).

9. Two wooden heads from the front end of the Nydam boat (AD 350).

10. Reconstruction of the village of Hjemsted around AD 450.

11. Descendants of Wearmud and Ongentheow.

12. Anglo-Saxon burial sites (Leeds 1970). "Anglo-Saxon" is a standard expression for Germanics living in Britain.

13. Descendants of Hrethel and Ecgtheof.

14. Gold bracteates found in Istathe Syssel and Holstein around AD 500.

15. Gold bracteate from Geltorf by the Schlei (Hauck cat. 254).

16. Descendants of Healfdene and Helm.

17. Gold bracteate from Undley near Lakenheath in Suffolk, around AD 500.

18. The reconstructed Anglian village at West Stow around AD 500.

19. Buckle from Galsted in Barwith Syssel, AD 400s.

20. Open-air idol from Oberdorla, Thüringia, height 32 cm, AD 200s.

21. Pots used for grave gifts.

a) Oberdorla, Thüringia, ca. AD 200 (Behm-Blancke 2002).

b) Hjemsted, southern Jutland, ca. AD 450 (Ethelberg 1986).

22. Urn from Spong Hill, North Elmham, Norfolk (Myres and Green 1973) and urn from Sancton, Yorkshire (Myres and Southern 1973), AD 400s.

23. Cruciform brooches, around AD 500: a) Olde, Norway; b) Dankirke, southern Jutland; c) Wakerley, North Hampshire (Hines 1984).

24. Square-headed brooch from Fairford, Luton. Guilt bronze. Drilled holes suggest repair in antiquity (Hines 1997).

25. Three sceattas of the so called Wodan/Monster type, AD 710.

26. Mythical eagle on the shield of Sutton Hoo. The face on the leg is copied.

27. Lid from a belt purse, where king Redwald kept his gold.

28. Part of a Scythian drinking horn from Merdjany, Kuban, Russia, 200s BC.

29. Sarmatian spearheads around AD 200 a) found in Dahmsdorf, near Berlin b) found in Kowel, northwest Ukraine (Shchukin 1994).

30. Buckle from Kossewen, Samland, around AD 200.

31. Wooden cup found in Vimose, on Funen, around AD 300.

32. Equal-armed brooch and two eagle brooches from a grave in Anderlingen, Haduloha, AD 400s (Hässler 1991).

33. Bronze strap ends from Abbeville by River Somme, AD 400s (Salin 1904).

34. Decoration on a brooch from Canterbury, Kent.

35. Pair of ornamented saucer brooches from a grave in Great Chesterford, Essex around AD 450 (Evison 1994).

36. Saucer brooches from North Wessex: a) East Shefford; b) Collingbourne Ducis (British Museum).

37. Disc brooch from Kingston, Kent, around AD 600.

39. Gable decorations in Lower Saxony called "Hengst and Hors", 1800s.

40. D-bracteates.
    a) from Grathe Hede, Jutland (Hauck cat.434b,1) and
    b) from Finglesham, Kent (Hauck cat.426,2b).

41. Bronze amulet in the form of a hammer from a grave in the Saxon cemetery at Ash, Kent (AD 500s).

42. The belt buckle from Finglesham, Kent, around AD 600.

42b. Sword pommel from the Staffordshire Hoard near Lichfield in Mercia.

43. The decoration of the upper seven rings of the long horn, based on Ole Worm's drawing.

44. Gold arm ring from a rich grave in Nordrup, Zealand; around AD 250.

45. Part of a sword sheath. Nydam Moor, Ellem Syssel, AD 350.

46. Cadeceus. The staff of Hermes.

47. Yin Yang symbol.

48. Stone ring used for religious ball playing by Mayans at Chicken-Itza, Mexico, AD 900.

49. Decoration plate of bronze from Niederursel, near Wiesbaden, Germany, AD 600s.

50. *Guldgubbe* from Helgö, Sweden and from Lundeborg, Funen, Denmark.

51. Franks Casket, the right side.

52. Carving at a gravestone from Gotland, around AD 500.

53. The "Spongman". Lid of an urn found at the Spong Hill cemetery.

54. The runic alphabet with pronunciation (second row) and the corresponding Venetic letters (third row).

55. Fibula from Meldorf, West Holstein, AD 40.

56. Gravestone from Wiesbaden.

57. The five rings from the short horn as recorded by Paulli.

58. Bronze bull with horns and silver eyes from Gudme on Funen, AD 300s.

59. Top of the whetstone sceptre from the Sutton Hoo ship burial.

60. Outline of the Red Horse of Tysoe, 76 x 61m.

61. Deer hunt. Stone carving from Bjergagergård, southern Jutland, 600 BC.

62. Bronze idols from Fårdal, Jutland, 600 BC.

63. Lance shaft with runic inscription from Kragehul Moor on Funen, AD 400s.

64. Stone heads with three faces from Glejbjerg and Bramminge, southern Jutland. The number "17" on the head from Bramminge is a later carving.

65. Urns from Funen, around AD 200. (a) Fraude; (b) Alenbækhuse (Albrechtsen 1968).66. Boar-crested helmet from Benty Grange in Derbyshire (Mercia) 600s.

66. Boar-crested helmet from Benty Grange in Derbyshire (Mercia), AD 600s.

67. The two uppermost rings of the short horn with the 24 sun symbols marked.

68. Ægishjalmr.

69. The human life cycle.

70. Runes in the east connected to the birth of man.

71. Runes in the northwest connected to the earth.

72. Runes in the north connected to the dead spirit.

73. Runes in the northeast connected to conception.

74. Runes in the southeast connected to the child.

75. Runes in the south connected to the worker.

76. Runes in the southwest connected to the ruler.

77. Runes in the west connected to death.

78. Sceatta found near Ipswich, East Anglia ca. AD 700 (Rickfors).

79. Drawing of the 18 sun marks of ring 3 on the long horn.

80. Idol of burned clay from Catalhöyük in Turkey.

81. Gold bracteate from Holmetorp, Öland, around AD 500 (Hauck cat.279).

82. Silver cups from Himlingøje, Zealand, around AD 275.

83. Figures from the Himlingøje Cups.

84. Wooden idol found in a well at Oss-Ussen, height 75 cm (Silkeborg 2001).

85. Gold bracteate from Gudme, Funen, around AD 500 (Hauck cat. 51,3).

86. Gold bracteate from Funen, AD 480s (Hauck cat. 58).

86b. Remains of the Uppåkra Temple.

87. Metal beaker with seven gold bands, AD 500s, found in Uppåkra.

88. Decoration on the gold bands of the metal beaker in figure 87.

89. Bracteate from Zealand (Hauck cat. 105).

90. Gold bracteate from Darum, near Ribe, in southwest Jutland, around AD 500 (Hauck cat. 42).

91. Sun-relief in the Church of Santa Maria Quintanilla de la Vinas, Burgos around AD 580.

92. An ølhøne from west Norway, 1800s.

93. Embroidered towel from North Zealand.

Bibliography

Ahrens, C., *Sachsen und Angelsachsen,* 1978.

Albrechtsen, E., *Fynske jernaldergrave,* 1968.

Axboe, M., *Brakteatstudier,* 2007.

Behm-Blancke, G., *Heiligtümer der Germanen und ihrer Vorgänger in Thüringen,* 2002.

Böhme, H.W., *Germanische Grabfunde des 4. bis 5. Jahrhunderts,* 1974.

Böhme, H.W., *Das ende der Romerherschaft in Britannien und die angelsachsische Besiedlung Englands im 5 Jahrhundert,* Jahrbuch des Römisch-Germanischen Zentral museum 33, 1986, p. 466-574.

Ethelberg, P., *Hjemsted,* 1986.

Evison, V.I., *The Fifth-Century Invasions South of the Thames,* 1965.

Evison, V.I., *Early Anglo-Saxon Applied Disc Brooches Part II: in England,* 1978.

Evison, V.I., *An Anglo Saxon Cemetery at Great Chesterford,* 1994.

Flowers, S., *The Galdrabok,* 1989.

Gimbutas, M., *The Language of the Goddess,* 2001.

Hamburishe Bericht e von Gelerthe Sachen 1774.

Hauck, K., *Die Goldbrakteaten der Völkerwanderungszeit.* 1985-1989.

Hills, C., *Who were the East Anglians?* East Anglian Archaeology Report no. 50, 1993, p. 14-23.

Hines, J., *The Scandinavian Character of Anglian England in the pre-Viking Period,* 1984.

Hines, J., *A New corpus of Anglo-Saxon Great Square-Headed Brooches,* 1997.

Hässler, H.J., *Das sächsische Gräberfeld bei Liebenau 2,* 1983.

Hässler, H.J., *Ur-und Frühgeschichte in Niedersachsen,* 1991.

Hodgkin, R.H., *A History of the Anglo-Saxons,* 1952.

Hope-Taylor, B., *Yeavering: an Anglo-British centre of Early Northumbria.* London. (Department of Environment Archaeological Reports 7), 1977.

Keys, D., *Catastrophe,* 2000.

Leeds, E.T., *The Archaeology of the Anglo-Saxon Settlements*, 1913 and 1970.

Larsson, L., *Uppåkra – Research on a Central Place*, Uppåkrastudier 6, 2002.

Myres and Green, *The Anglo-Saxon Cemeteries of Caistor-by-Norwich*, 1973.

Myres and Southern, *The Anglo-Saxon Cremation Cemetery at Sancton*, 1973.

Myres, J.N.L., *The English Settlements*, 1986.

Newton, S., *The Origins of Beowulf and the Pre-Viking Kingdom of East Anglia*, 1993.

Oxenstierna, E., *Die Goldhörner von Gallehus*, 1956.

Rasmussen, F., *Guldhornenes tydning*, 1990.

Rasmussen, F., www.finse.dk/ugarit 1997.

Rasmussen, F., *Germanerne og vikingerne*, 2004.

Rasmussen, F., www.finse.dk/franks casket.htm 2005

Rasmussen, F., *Nyt syn på Trelleborgene*, 2006.

Rickors, F., www.verasir.dk

Silkeborg museum, *Immortal image*, 2001.

Salin, B., *Die altgermanische Thierornamentik*, 1904.

Slade, B., http://www.heorot.dk/beowulf-rede-text.html 2002.

Saxo, https://en.wikisource.org/wiki/The_Danish_History

Shchukin, M., *Shields, swords and spears as evidence of Germanic-Sarmatian contacts and Barbarian-Roman relations*, 1994.

Walton, Rogers. *Tyttel's Halh: The Anglo-Saxon Cemetery at Tittleshall, Norfolk*, 2013.

Ward, D., *The Divine Twins: an Indo-European Myth in Germanic Tradition*, Folklore Studies 19, 1968.

Wallis, F., *Bede: The Reckoning of Time*, 1999.

Weale, M.E. *et.al.*, Y *Chromosome Evidence for Anglo-Saxon Mass Migration (2002)*.

http://mbe.oxfordjournals.org/cgi/reprint/19/7/1008

Wüttke, H., *Aithikos' Kosmographie*, 1853.

www.ingramcontent.com/pod-product-compliance
Lightning Source LLC
Chambersburg PA
CBHW040411110426
42812CB00012B/2521